# Exploring Time Travel

## Unmasking Time's Hidden Potentials

Peter Kattan

Petra Books
www.petrabooks.com

Exploring Time Travel
Unmasking Time's Hidden Potentials

To contact the author send email to:
pkattan@petrabooks.com

---

Exploring Time Travel: Unmasking Time's Hidden Potentials, written by Peter I. Kattan.

ISBN: 979-8-8691-6450-6

## Preface

Within the pages of this book we embark on an odyssey that transcends the mundane confines of everyday existence. In this anthology, we delve into the profound mysteries of time—its secret potential, its enigmatic allure, and its infinite possibilities.

At the heart of our exploration lies the tantalizing concept of time travel. The chapter on "Time Travel Dilemmas" beckons us to ponder the ethical quandaries and paradoxes inherent in traversing the temporal landscape, while "Problem-Solving through Time Travel" offers a glimpse into the practical applications of this extraordinary phenomenon.

Guided by the beacon of scientific inquiry, we navigate the intricate web of temporal dynamics, seeking to unravel the very fabric of time itself. "Unraveling the Science of Time Travel" takes us on a journey through the cutting-edge research and theoretical frameworks that underpin our understanding of temporal mechanics, illuminating the path towards new frontiers of knowledge.

Yet, our exploration does not end with the confines of our own timeline. "Time Travel and Multiverse Theories" invites us to contemplate the mind-bending concept of parallel universes and the profound implications they hold for our understanding of reality.

As we venture deeper into the temporal abyss, we confront the notion of causality and the delicate balance that governs the ripple effects of our actions. "Ripples in the Fabric of Time Travel" serves as a poignant reminder of the interconnectedness of past, present, and future, urging us to tread lightly as we navigate the currents of time.

And yet, despite the myriad challenges and uncertainties that lie ahead, we are filled with a sense of boundless optimism. For within the evolving landscape of time travel, we find not just the promise of discovery, but also the potential to shape our own destiny.

So, dear reader, let us embark together on this extraordinary journey through the corridors of time. For in the pages that follow, you will find not just a collection of ideas and insights, but a testament to the enduring human spirit of curiosity, exploration, and the relentless pursuit of knowledge.

Peter Kattan

# Contents

Exploring Time Travel
Unmasking Time's Hidden Potentials

# 1. Time's Secret Potential

Time travel is one of the most fascinating and intriguing concepts that has ever captured the imagination of people from all walks of life. It has been a popular theme in science fiction for many years, with many books, movies, and TV shows exploring the possibilities of time travel. While time travel remains firmly in the realm of science fiction, there are some intriguing possibilities that have been explored by physicists and other experts.

One of the most fascinating possibilities of time travel is the idea of the grandfather paradox. This paradox suggests that if someone were to travel back in time and kill their own grandfather, they would prevent their own existence. The paradox highlights the potential dangers and paradoxes of time travel. If time travel were possible, it could lead to all kinds of paradoxes and complications, making it difficult to navigate and understand.

Despite the potential dangers and paradoxes of time travel, scientists and researchers continue to explore the concept. By better understanding the nature of time and how it interacts with space and matter, we may one day be able to unlock the secrets of time travel and explore the unseen possibilities of the past and future.

The concept of time travel has been around for centuries, with many scientists and philosophers exploring the possibilities and implications of time travel. Some of the earliest examples of time travel can be found in ancient literature, such as the Greek myth of Chronos and the Hindu myth of King Kakudmi. In these stories, characters travel through time to different eras and meet people from different times.

However, it was not until the 19th century that the idea of time travel began to take shape in a more scientific and mathematical way. In 1895, H.G. Wells published his classic novel "The Time Machine," which introduced the concept of a machine that could travel through time. The book was a huge success and helped to popularize the idea of time travel.

Since then, the concept of time travel has been explored by many scientists and researchers. The most famous example is perhaps Albert Einstein, whose theory of relativity introduced the idea that time can be stretched or compressed depending on the observer's frame of reference. While Einstein's theory did not explicitly deal with time travel, it did lay the groundwork for future researchers to explore the concept.

One of the most intriguing possibilities of time travel is the idea of closed timelike curves. These are paths through spacetime that return to their starting point, allowing a person to travel back in time and interact with their younger self. While closed timelike curves are purely theoretical at this point, they provide a tantalizing glimpse into the possibilities of time travel.

The idea of closed timelike curves was first proposed by physicist Kurt Gödel in 1949. Gödel suggested that if the universe were rotating, it could create a closed timelike curve, which would allow time travel. While Gödel's idea has not been proven, it has inspired many researchers to explore the possibilities of closed timelike curves and other theoretical concepts.

Another concept that has been explored by researchers is the idea of wormholes. Wormholes are hypothetical structures that could connect two different points in space-time, allowing for faster-than-light travel and potentially time travel. While wormholes are purely theoretical at this point, they have captured the imagination of many scientists and science fiction writers.

Despite the many paradoxes and potential dangers of time travel, scientists and researchers continue to explore the concept. They hope to better understand the nature of time and how it interacts with space and matter, and to one day unlock the secrets of time travel.

Despite the many paradoxes and potential dangers of time travel, scientists and researchers continue to explore the concept. By better understanding the nature of time and how it interacts with space and matter, we may one day be able to unlock the secrets of time travel and explore the unseen possibilities of the past and future.

The idea of being able to travel back and forth through time, exploring different eras and events, has captured the imaginations of people from all walks of life. Despite the fact that time travel remains firmly in the realm of science fiction, there are some intriguing possibilities that have been explored by physicists and other experts.

The idea of time travel is not a new one. It has been around for centuries and has been the subject of countless works of fiction. From H.G. Wells' "The Time Machine" to the "Back to the Future" film franchise, people have been captivated by the idea of traveling through time. But while these stories are entertaining, they are purely works of fiction.

The grandfather paradox is a well-known problem in time travel. The paradox is essentially a question of causality. If someone were to travel back in time and prevent their own birth, then they would not be able to travel back in time in the first place. This creates a paradox that cannot be resolved. It is a problem that has plagued time travel fiction for decades, but it is also a problem that scientists and researchers have been trying to solve.

One solution to the grandfather paradox is the idea of the parallel universe. According to this theory, every time someone travels back in time and changes something, a new parallel universe is created. This means that the person who traveled back in time would be in a different universe than the one they came from, and they would not have prevented their own birth. This solution has been explored in many works of science fiction, including the popular TV show "Doctor Who."

The concept of closed timelike curves was first proposed by the physicist Kurt Gödel in 1949. Gödel showed that a rotating universe could have closed timelike curves, which would allow for time travel. However, the idea was not taken seriously at the time, and it was largely forgotten until the 1960s when physicist Frank Tipler rediscovered Gödel's work.

One of the key challenges in understanding time travel is the nature of time itself. Time is a fundamental part of our experience of the world, but it is also one of the most mysterious. According to the theory of relativity, time is not absolute but is relative to the observer. This means that time can move slower or faster depending on the observer's speed and location.

The relationship between time and space is also a key area of research. According to the theory of relativity, space and time are not separate entities but are intertwined in a single concept called spacetime. This means that any event that occurs in space also occurs in time, and any change n space also affects time. This is why time can be affected by gravity, and why time can slow down near massive objects such as black holes.

The nature of time and space-time is also being explored in the context of quantum mechanics. In quantum mechanics, particles can exist in multiple states simultaneously, a concept known as superposition. This means that time and space can also exist in multiple states simultaneously, which could have implications for time travel.

One theory of time travel involves the use of wormholes. A wormhole is a theoretical passage through space-time that would allow a person to travel from one point in space-time to another, potentially traveling through time as well. Wormholes are predicted by the equations of general relativity, but their existence has not been confirmed.

The idea of using wormholes for time travel was popularized by the physicist Kip Thorne, who worked as a consultant on the film "Interstellar." In the film, a spaceship travels through a wormhole to explore a distant galaxy, but the crew also experiences time dilation, meaning that time moves more slowly for them than for people on Earth.

While the idea of using wormholes for time travel is intriguing, it is also highly speculative. There are many challenges to the concept, including the fact that wormholes would need to be stabilized and traversable, and that they could potentially lead to dangerous paradoxes.

Despite the challenges and uncertainties surrounding time travel, the concept continues to fascinate and inspire people. In addition to being a popular subject in science fiction, time travel has also been explored in academic and philosophical circles. Some philosophers have argued that time travel is impossible because it violates the laws of causality, while others have suggested that time travel could be possible but would require a radically different understanding of time and space.

The possibility of time travel also raises important ethical questions. If time travel were possible, what would be the implications for our understanding of history and causality? Could time travel be used to prevent tragedies or alter the course of history, and if so, should it be allowed? These are complex questions that require careful consideration and discussion.

In conclusion, time travel remains a fascinating and complex concept that continues to capture the imaginations of people from all walks of life. While time travel remains firmly in the realm of science fiction, there are some intriguing possibilities that have been explored by physicists and other experts. The grandfather paradox, closed timelike curves, wormholes, and parallel universes are just a few of the many concepts that have been explored in the context of time travel.

Despite the many paradoxes and potential dangers of time travel, scientists and researchers continue to explore the concept, driven by a desire to better understand the nature of time and space. As our understanding of the universe continues to evolve, it is possible that we may one day be able to unlock the secrets of time travel and explore the unseen possibilities of the past and future. However, it is important to approach the concept with caution and to carefully consider the ethical and philosophical implications of time travel.

One potential application of time travel, if it were possible, could be in studying the history of our planet and the universe. By traveling back in time, scientists could observe key events in Earth's history, such as the formation of the first life forms, the extinction of the dinosaurs, and the evolution of humans. Similarly, time travel could be used to explore the origins of the universe, including the Big Bang and the formation of galaxies and stars.

Time travel could also have practical applications in fields such as archaeology, where it could be used to study ancient civilizations and artifacts, and in medicine, where it could be used to study the progression of diseases over time.

However, it is important to note that these applications are purely speculative at this point and would require a much deeper understanding of the nature of time and space before they could become a reality.

Another potential implication of time travel is in the realm of causality. If time travel were possible, it would raise important questions about the nature of cause and effect. For example, if someone were to travel back in time and change a key event, such as the assassination of a historical figure, what would be the implications for the future? Would the timeline split off into a parallel universe, or would the changes ripple through time, altering the course of history in unforeseen ways?

These questions highlight the potential dangers and ethical considerations that would need to be taken into account if time travel were ever to become a reality. In addition to the potential for causing harm by altering the timeline, there is also the risk of creating paradoxes, such as the grandfather paradox mentioned earlier.

Despite these challenges, many scientists and researchers continue to explore the concept of time travel, driven by a desire to better understand the nature of time and space. This research has led to many intriguing discoveries, including the concept of time dilation, which states that time moves more slowly for objects that are moving at high speeds or are in strong gravitational fields.

In addition, scientists have also made significant progress in developing theories of quantum mechanics and the nature of the universe, which could have important implications for time travel. For example, the concept of entanglement, in which particles can be connected in ways that defy classical physics, could have implications for time travel and the nature of causality.

Time travel has long been a fascination for people from all walks of life, whether it is through movies, books or simply daydreaming. The concept of being able to travel back and forth through time, exploring different eras and events, has captured the imaginations of many. Despite the fact that time travel is still in the realm of science fiction, there are some intriguing possibilities that have been explored by physicists and other experts.

One of the most fascinating aspects of time travel is the idea of the grandfather paradox. This paradox suggests that if someone were to travel back in time and kill their own grandfather, they would prevent their own existence. The paradox highlights the potential dangers and paradoxes of time travel. The paradox is based on the idea that time travel would allow someone to alter the past, and therefore, alter the present and future. If someone were to travel back in time and alter a key event, such as killing their own grandfather, they would be altering the course of history and potentially preventing their own existence. This is a classic example of the paradox of time travel.

The idea of the grandfather paradox is not just a thought experiment; it is actually a real problem that has been explored by physicists and other experts. One solution to the paradox is the many-worlds interpretation of quantum mechanics, which suggests that every possible outcome of a quantum event actually occurs in a separate universe. In this interpretation, if someone were to travel back in time and kill their own grandfather, they would simply create a new universe where they never existed.

Another intriguing possibility of time travel is the idea of closed timelike curves. These are paths through spacetime that return to their starting point, allowing a person to travel back in time and interact with their younger self. While closed timelike curves are purely theoretical at this point, they provide a tantalizing glimpse into the possibilities of time travel.

The idea of closed timelike curves is based on the theory of general relativity, which describes the nature of gravity and the geometry of spacetime. According to this theory, spacetime is curved by the presence of matter and energy. The curvature of spacetime determines the path of objects moving through it, including light and other particles. The idea of a closed timelike curve suggests that it might be possible to create a path through spacetime that loops back on itself, allowing someone to travel back in time.

While the idea of closed timelike curves is intriguing, it also raises a number of paradoxes and questions. For example, if someone were to travel back in time and change a key event, such as preventing the assassination of a political leader, what would be the consequences for the present and future? Would the person who traveled back in time still exist in the altered timeline, or would they be erased from existence? These are complex and difficult questions that have yet to be answered.

One way that scientists are exploring the concept of time travel is through the study of black holes. Black holes are incredibly dense objects that warp the fabric of spacetime around them. According to the theory of general relativity, time moves more slowly in regions of strong gravity. This means that time moves more slowly near a black hole than it does in other parts of the universe.

Some scientists have proposed that it might be possible to use the extreme gravity of a black hole to create a closed timelike curve. According to this theory, if someone were to orbit a black hole at a certain distance and then return to their starting point, they would find themselves in the past. This is because the intense gravitational pull of the black hole would cause time to slow down, allowing the person to effectively travel back in time.

However, this theory is not without its own set of paradoxes and potential dangers. For example, if someone were to travel back in time and change a key event, such as preventing a disaster or altering a historical event, the consequences for the present and future could be catastrophic. This is because altering the past would fundamentally change the course of history, potentially creating a new timeline where everything is different.

Despite the potential dangers, the study of black holes and their effects on spacetime is one of the most promising avenues for exploring the concept of time travel. By better understanding the nature of black holes and how they interact with spacetime, scientists may one day be able to unlock the secrets of time travel and explore the unseen possibilities of the past and future.

Another area of research that is gaining momentum in the study of time travel is the development of quantum computers. Quantum computers are based on the principles of quantum mechanics, which describe the behavior of particles at the subatomic level. Unlike traditional computers, which use bits to represent information, quantum computers use quantum bits, or qubits, which can exist in multiple states at the same time.

One of the unique properties of quantum mechanics is the idea of entanglement. Entanglement occurs when two particles become linked in such a way that the state of one particle is dependent on the state of the other, regardless of the distance between them. This phenomenon has been used to develop quantum teleportation, where information can be transmitted instantly between two entangled particles, regardless of the distance between them.

Scientists have proposed that quantum computers could be used to simulate the effects of time travel. By using qubits to simulate the effects of time dilation, it might be possible to study the effects of time travel without actually physically traveling through time. This approach would allow scientists to explore the potential dangers and paradoxes of time travel in a controlled environment, without the risk of altering the course of history.

Time travel remains one of the most fascinating and tantalizing concepts in science and popular culture. Despite the many paradoxes and potential dangers associated with time travel, scientists and researchers continue to explore the concept. By better understanding the nature of time and how it interacts with space and matter, we may one day be able to unlock the secrets of time travel and explore the unseen possibilities of the past and future. From the study of black holes to the development of quantum computers, there are many promising avenues for exploring the concept of time travel. While we may never be able to physically travel through time, the study of time travel continues to push the boundaries of our understanding of the universe and our place in it.

## 2. Navigating Temporal Realms

Time is one of the most fundamental concepts in the universe, yet it remains one of the most mysterious. Scientists and researchers have long grappled with the nature of time, exploring its properties and how it interacts with space and matter.

One of the key insights into the nature of time comes from the theory of relativity. According to this theory, time can be influenced by the presence of mass and energy, leading to phenomena like time dilation and time travel.

Despite the many mysteries surrounding the nature of time, researchers continue to make breakthroughs in our understanding of this fundamental concept. By unlocking the secrets of time, we may be able to explore new frontiers and uncover the unseen possibilities of the universe.

Time, one of the most fundamental concepts in the universe, has remained one of the most mysterious. Scientists and researchers have long grappled with the nature of time, exploring its properties and how it interacts with space and matter. From the beginning of human civilization, people have been fascinated by the concept of time. However, despite thousands of years of study, the true nature of time remains a mystery. In this article, we will explore the concept of time, including how it interacts with space and matter, how it can be influenced by mass and energy, the theory of relativity, the concept of time crystals, and breakthroughs in our understanding of time.

Time is a fundamental concept in the universe, and it is a measurement of the duration between events. The concept of time is essential in our daily lives, from scheduling appointments to measuring the age of the universe. The measurement of time is based on the rotation of the Earth, and it is divided into units, including seconds, minutes, hours, days, weeks, months, and years.

The concept of time is also closely related to the concept of space. The two concepts are interconnected, and they form the basis of the concept of spacetime. Spacetime is the four-dimensional continuum that combines space and time. In this framework, space and time are not separate entities but are interconnected and inseparable. The concept of spacetime was first proposed by Albert Einstein in his theory of relativity.

The theory of relativity is one of the most significant scientific achievements in human history. The theory, proposed by Albert Einstein in 1905, transformed our understanding of the nature of time and space. According to the theory of relativity, time can be influenced by the presence of mass and energy, leading to phenomena like time dilation and time travel.

One of the key insights into the nature of time from the theory of relativity is the concept of time dilation. Time dilation is the phenomenon that occurs when time appears to pass more slowly in a gravitational field or in a moving object. This phenomenon is a consequence of the fact that time and space are interconnected and that the speed of light is constant.

Another phenomenon predicted by the theory of relativity is time travel. Time travel is a concept that has fascinated humans for centuries, and it is a staple of science fiction. While time travel is still a hypothetical concept, the theory of relativity suggests that it may be possible under certain conditions. For example, if an object could travel faster than the speed of light, it could theoretically travel back in time.

Another area of research into the science of time is the concept of time crystals. Time crystals are materials that exhibit periodic motion in time, rather than space. While still a relatively new area of study, time crystals could have a wide range of potential applications, from quantum computing to precision timekeeping.

The concept of time crystals was first proposed by Frank Wilczek, a physicist at the Massachusetts Institute of Technology. According to Wilczek's theory, time crystals are materials that exhibit periodic motion in time, just as crystals exhibit periodic motion in space. In other words, time crystals are materials that oscillate between different states in a predictable pattern, without the need for any external influencc.

Despite the many mysteries surrounding the nature of time, researchers continue to make breakthroughs in our understanding of this fundamental concept. For example, in 2017, a team of physicists at the University of California, Berkeley, announced that they had created the world's first time crystal. The time crystal created by the team was made of a diamond, and it exhibited a periodic motion in time.

Albert Einstein's theory of relativity revolutionized our understanding of time and space. According to this theory, time is not absolute, but rather depends on the observer's frame of reference. In other words, time is relative to the observer's position and motion.

One of the key insights of the theory of relativity is time dilation. Time dilation is the phenomenon in which time appears to pass slower in a gravitational field or when an object is moving at high speeds. This effect has been experimentally verified and has important implications for space travel and the study of black holes.

The discovery of time crystals is a relatively new area of study, with the first examples being created in 2016. Since then, researchers have been exploring the potential applications of these materials, which could have a wide range of uses in fields such as quantum computing and precision timekeeping.

One of the most exciting implications of time crystals is their potential use in quantum computing. Because time crystals exhibit periodic motion, they could be used to create a stable clock signal for quantum computers, which require precise synchronization between their different components.

Time crystals also have potential applications in precision timekeeping. Because they exhibit a stable and periodic motion, they could be used to create ultra-precise clocks and timers, which could have important applications in fields such as navigation and communications.

Despite the many breakthroughs in our understanding of time, there are still many mysteries surrounding this fundamental concept. For example, the question of why time moves forward, rather than backward, remains a subject of intense study and debate.

Researchers are also exploring the possibility of other exotic phenomena related to time, such as the existence of closed timelike curves, which would allow for time travel without violating the laws of physics.

By unlocking the secrets of time, researchers hope to gain new insights into the nature of the universe and explore new frontiers in science and technology. Whether through the study of time dilation and time travel, or the exploration of time crystals and other exotic phenomena, the science of time remains a subject of intense study and fascination.

Recent breakthroughs in the study of time have opened up new avenues of research, and scientists are continuing to push the boundaries of our understanding of this fundamental concept. One area of ongoing research is the study of time and consciousness. Some researchers have suggested that our subjective experience of time is intimately linked to our perception of consciousness.

Other scientists are exploring the possibility of time travel and its potential implications for the future of humanity. While time travel remains a subject of science fiction, researchers are studying the theoretical possibilities and exploring ways to make it a reality.

One of the most exciting areas of research in the study of time is the development of new technologies that could revolutionize our understanding of the universe. For example, researchers are developing ultra-precise clocks and timers that are capable of measuring time to within a billionth of a second.

These ultra-precise time measurements could have important applications in fields such as astronomy, where accurate timekeeping is essential for measuring the distances between celestial bodies and studying the evolution of the universe.

Other potential applications of ultra-precise time measurements include the development of new technologies for communication and navigation. For example, ultra-precise clocks could be used to synchronize the signals in communication networks, leading to faster and more reliable communication.

Similarly, ultra-precise time measurements could be used in navigation systems to improve the accuracy of GPS and other positioning technologies. This could have important applications in fields such as transportation, where accurate positioning is essential for safety and efficiency.

Despite these breakthroughs, many mysteries still surround the nature of time, and researchers continue to push the boundaries of our knowledge in this area. By unlocking the secrets of time, we may be able to explore new frontiers and uncover the unseen possibilities of the universe.

Moreover, time is not only a fundamental concept in science, but it is also a crucial factor in our daily lives. We all have a subjective experience of time, which is influenced by various factors such as age, attention, and emotional state. Time is a resource that we can never get back, and managing it effectively is essential for productivity, happiness, and success.

As we continue to learn more about time, we are also learning more about ourselves and our place in the universe. Understanding the nature of time and how it influences our perception of reality could have important implications for fields such as psychology, neuroscience, and philosophy.

For example, some researchers have suggested that our subjective experience of time could be linked to our perception of free will. If our experience of time is malleable, then perhaps our sense of agency and the choices we make are also malleable.

Similarly, the study of time could shed light on the nature of consciousness and the relationship between the mind and the body. Some researchers have suggested that time and consciousness are intimately linked, and that understanding the nature of time could help us unravel the mysteries of the mind.

In addition to its applications in science and technology, the study of time also has cultural and philosophical implications. Time is a concept that is central to many human cultures, and it has inspired countless works of art, literature, and philosophy throughout history.

For example, the concept of time has been explored in works such as Marcel Proust's "In Search of Lost Time," James Joyce's "Ulysses," and the films of Stanley Kubrick. Time is also a central theme in many philosophical traditions, from ancient Greek philosophy to contemporary existentialism.

One of the most revolutionary ideas in the science of time came from the theory of relativity, developed by Albert Einstein in the early 20th century. This theory postulated that the passage of time can be influenced by the presence of mass and energy. According to this theory, time can be distorted or stretched in the presence of massive objects or high energy densities.

This phenomenon is known as time dilation. Time dilation occurs because time is not a universal constant, as previously thought. Instead, it is relative to the observer's frame of reference. The faster an object moves or the more massive it is, the more time appears to slow down for observers in other frames of reference. This effect has been observed in many experiments, including the Hafele-Keating experiment, which used atomic clocks to measure the effects of time dilation during commercial airline flights.

The theory of relativity has also led to the possibility of time travel. While still a subject of science fiction, the idea of time travel is not ruled out by the laws of physics. According to Einstein's theory, time travel is possible if an object can travel faster than the speed of light. However, this remains a theoretical concept, as achieving such speeds is currently beyond our technological capabilities.

Another area of research into the science of time is the concept of time crystals. Unlike traditional crystals, which exhibit periodic motion in space, time crystals exhibit periodic motion in time. In other words, they repeat their motion in time rather than in space. This concept was first proposed in 2012 by Nobel laureate Frank Wilczek.

Time crystals are made up of a series of atoms or particles that are arranged in a repeating pattern. Unlike traditional crystals, time crystals do not require any external energy to maintain their motion, making them an intriguing subject of study. While still in their infancy, time crystals could have a wide range of potential applications, including in quantum computing and precision timekeeping.

One potential application of time crystals is in quantum computing. Quantum computers rely on the manipulation of quantum bits or qubits, which are highly sensitive to environmental disturbances. Time crystals, with their stable and repeating patterns, could provide a more stable and predictable environment for quantum computing operations. This could potentially lead to faster and more efficient quantum computing systems.

Another potential application of time crystals is in precision timekeeping. Traditional atomic clocks, which rely on the vibrations of atoms to keep time, are highly accurate but can be affected by external factors such as temperature and magnetic fields. Time crystals, with their stable and predictable motion, could provide a more accurate and reliable method of timekeeping.

Despite the many mysteries surrounding the nature of time, researchers continue to make breakthroughs in our understanding of this fundamental concept. The study of time is interdisciplinary, with contributions from physics, mathematics, and philosophy. By unlocking the secrets of time, we may be able to explore new frontiers and uncover the unseen possibilities of the universe.

One area of research that could shed light on the mysteries of time is quantum gravity. This field seeks to unify the laws of quantum mechanics and general relativity, which govern the behavior of matter and energy in the universe. By understanding the fundamental nature of time at a quantum level, we may be able to unravel some of the most perplexing questions about the nature of the universe, including the nature of black holes and the origin of the universe itself.

Another area of research that could contribute to our understanding of time is the study of the brain. The perception of time is a subjective experience, and our perception of time can vary depending on our emotional state and other factors. By understanding the neural mechanisms that underlie our perception of time, we may be able to gain a deeper insight into the nature of time and how it relates to consciousness.

The study of time is not only of interest to scientists and researchers but also to philosophers and theologians. Questions about the nature of time and its relationship to free will, determinism, and the concept of eternity have been debated for centuries. The study of time raises fundamental questions about the nature of reality and our place in the universe.

Time is a mysterious and fundamental concept that has intrigued scientists and researchers for centuries. The study of time encompasses a wide range of disciplines, including physics, mathematics, philosophy, and neuroscience. Through the study of time, we have gained new insights into the nature of the universe, including the concept of time dilation and the potential applications of time crystals.

Furthermore, the study of time has practical applications as well. Accurate timekeeping is essential for many fields, from GPS navigation to financial transactions. The development of atomic clocks, which measure time using the vibrations of atoms, has revolutionized our ability to measure time accurately and precisely.

In addition, our understanding of time has implications for the development of technologies such as quantum computing. The behavior of quantum systems is strongly influenced by time, and a deeper understanding of the nature of time could lead to more efficient and powerful quantum computers.

The study of time also has philosophical implications. Questions about the nature of time and its relationship to causality and determinism have been debated for centuries. The concept of free will is closely tied to our understanding of time, and the study of time has the potential to shed light on this complex and controversial topic.

Furthermore, the study of time raises questions about the nature of reality itself. Is time an objective feature of the universe, or is it a product of our subjective experience? What is the relationship between time and space, and how does time relate to the structure of the universe as a whole?

These are profound questions that touch on some of the most fundamental aspects of our existence, and the study of time provides a framework for exploring them. By unlocking the mysteries of time, we may be able to gain a deeper understanding of the nature of reality and our place in the universe.

Time is a fundamental and mysterious concept that has captivated the imaginations of scientists, philosophers, and theologians for centuries. From the theory of relativity to the study of time crystals, the study of time encompasses a wide range of disciplines and has implications for our understanding of the universe, the development of technology, and the nature of reality itself.

Despite the many breakthroughs in our understanding of time, many mysteries remain, and the study of time continues to be an active and exciting field of research. By unlocking the secrets of time, we may be able to explore new frontiers and uncover the unseen possibilities of the universe.

## 3.  Time Travel Dilemmas

While time travel remains firmly in the realm of science fiction, the concept raises a host of ethical considerations. From altering the course of history to potentially changing the outcome of events, time travel has the potential to disrupt the natural order of things in profound ways.

One of the most pressing ethical considerations surrounding time travel is the question of historical authenticity. If someone were to travel back in time and alter the course of history, would it still be considered authentic? Would we lose something essential if events were changed, even if they were changed for the better?

 Another ethical concern is the potential impact on future generations. If we were able to change the past through time travel, what would be the implications for those who come after us? Would they still exist, or would the changes we made in the past create a new reality that they have no connection to? There is also the question of accountability. If someone were to travel back in time and commit a crime or cause harm, who would be held responsible? Would they be held accountable in the past or the present? And how would justice be served in a situation where the rules of time and space are no longer applicable?
Despite the many ethical considerations, there are also potential benefits to time travel. For example, it could allow us to witness historical events firsthand or help us to better understand the evolution of our species. However, these benefits must be weighed against the potential risks and consequences of meddling with the natural order of time and space.

Overall, the ethics of time travel is a complex and multifaceted topic that requires careful consideration and examination. As we continue to explore the possibilities of time travel, it is important that we do so with a thoughtful and ethical approach that takes into account the potential impact on the past, present, and future.

Time travel is a concept that has fascinated humans for centuries. The idea of being able to go back in time or into the future has been explored extensively in science fiction literature and movies, but in reality, time travel remains firmly in the realm of science fiction. However, the concept of time travel raises a host of ethical considerations that are worth exploring.

One of the most pressing ethical considerations surrounding time travel is the question of historical authenticity. If someone were to travel back in time and alter the course of history, would it still be considered authentic? Would we lose something essential if events were changed, even if they were changed for the better? For example, if someone were to go back in time and prevent a significant historical event from occurring, such as the assassination of President John F. Kennedy, would it change the course of history in unforeseeable ways? Would we be living in a completely different world today if that event had not occurred? These are challenging questions that require serious consideration.

Another ethical concern is the potential impact on future generations. If we were able to change the past through time travel, what would be the implications for those who come after us? Would they still exist, or would the changes we made in the past create a new reality that they have no connection to? For example, if someone were to go back in time and prevent their grandparents from meeting, would their parents and then they themselves cease to exist? The ripple effects of time travel could be far-reaching and unpredictable, making it essential to consider the potential impact on future generations.

There is also the question of accountability. If someone were to travel back in time and commit a crime or cause harm, who would be held responsible? Would they be held accountable in the past or the present? And how would justice be served in a situation where the rules of time and space are no longer applicable? For example, if someone were to travel back in time and kill someone, would they be tried and punished in the present for a crime committed in the past? These questions raise complex ethical and legal considerations that must be addressed.

Despite the many ethical considerations, there are also potential benefits to time travel. For example, it could allow us to witness historical events firsthand or help us to better understand the evolution of our species. Imagine being able to travel back in time and see the construction of the pyramids or witness the signing of the Declaration of Independence. Time travel could also allow us to gain a better understanding of the origins of our species and the evolution of human society.

However, these benefits must be weighed against the potential risks and consequences of meddling with the natural order of time and space. The possibility of altering the course of history, creating a new reality, or causing harm to oneself or others is significant. Additionally, the impact on future generations cannot be overlooked.

Another ethical consideration related to time travel is the question of consent. If someone were to travel back in time and interact with people from the past, would they be infringing on their rights? For example, if someone were to travel back in time and meet a historical figure, would that person have given consent to that interaction? Would the person from the past have been able to give informed consent to the interaction, given that they would have no understanding of the concept of time travel?

Furthermore, there is the question of privilege. Time travel is a technology that would likely only be available to a privileged few, raising concerns about inequality and access. Those who are able to time travel would have access to experiences and information that others do not, creating a further divide between the haves and have-nots.

Time travel has long been a popular topic in science fiction, but despite the abundance of books, movies, and TV shows that explore the concept, time travel remains firmly in the realm of fantasy. However, just because time travel is currently impossible does not mean that we should not consider its potential implications. Indeed, the very fact that time travel is impossible makes it an ideal subject for ethical speculation, precisely because it raises questions that we cannot answer with empirical data.

One of the most pressing ethical considerations surrounding time travel is the question of historical authenticity. If someone were to travel back in time and alter the course of history, would it still be considered authentic? This is a complex question, as the answer depends on what one means by "authentic." If we define authenticity as fidelity to the facts, then changing the course of history would obviously violate this principle. However, if we define authenticity as something more abstract, such as a sense of cultural continuity or a feeling of belonging to a shared historical narrative, then the answer is less clear.

Consider, for example, the hypothetical scenario in which a time traveler goes back in time and prevents the assassination of Archduke Franz Ferdinand, thus preventing the outbreak of World War I. On the one hand, we might say that this would be a positive development, as it would spare millions of lives and prevent untold suffering. On the other hand, we might also say that this would be a loss, as the experience of World War I is an essential part of our collective historical memory. Would we lose something essential if events were changed, even if they were changed for the better?

This is not just an abstract question. In recent years, there has been a growing movement to remove statues and monuments that celebrate figures with problematic histories. For example, in the United States, there has been controversy over Confederate statues, which many people argue should be removed because they celebrate figures who fought to preserve slavery. However, others argue that removing these statues erases an essential part of our history, and that it is important to remember and acknowledge the mistakes of the past.

Another ethical concern surrounding time travel is the potential impact on future generations. If we were able to change the past through time travel, what would be the implications for those who come after us? Would they still exist, or would the changes we made in the past create a new reality that they have no connection to? This question raises a host of philosophical and metaphysical issues. For example, if time travel were possible, would it be possible to create a paradox in which a person goes back in time and kills their own grandfather, thus preventing their own birth? This is known as the grandfather paradox, and it has been the subject of much debate among philosophers and physicists.

This question is not merely theoretical. In 2016, a man named Robert Franklin was charged with bigamy after he married a woman in 2010, then traveled back in time to 1988 and married another woman without first getting a divorce. The case raised a number of difficult legal questions, such as whether the bigamy charge applied to the 1988 marriage, and whether Franklin could be held responsible for a crime that occurred before the law was passed.

Of course, these are all hypothetical scenarios, and it is impossible to know for sure how time travel would actually work, or what its implications would be. However, the fact that these questions are being asked at all is a testament to the enduring fascination with the idea of time travel and the importance of considering the ethical implications of new technologies and scientific advancements.

Another ethical issue raised by time travel is the potential for unintended consequences. As the butterfly effect famously demonstrates, even small changes to the past can have significant ripple effects on the future. For example, if a time traveler were to go back in time and prevent a natural disaster, they might inadvertently cause a different disaster in its place. Similarly, if a time traveler were to go back in time and prevent a famous author from dying prematurely, they might inadvertently change the course of literary history by preventing them from writing their most famous works.

This potential for unintended consequences raises the question of whether time travel is a responsible technology to develop. As with any new technology, it is important to weigh the potential benefits against the potential risks. While time travel has the potential to solve many of humanity's problems, it also has the potential to create new problems that we cannot yet imagine.

Perhaps the most profound ethical consideration raised by time travel is the question of whether we have the right to change the course of history. From an ethical standpoint, there is a strong argument to be made that we have a responsibility to preserve the natural order of things, even if that order is not always ideal. Changing the past is a kind of hubris, as it assumes that we know better than the people who actually lived through those events.

This idea is explored in the classic science fiction novel The Time Machine by H.G. Wells. In the novel, the protagonist travels far into the future and discovers that humanity has evolved into two distinct species: the peaceful and childlike Eloi, and the violent and brutish Morlocks. The protagonist is horrified by what he sees and decides to go back in time and prevent the evolution of these two species. However, when he returns to his own time, he discovers that his meddling has had unintended consequences, and that the world is even worse off than it was before.

The Time Machine is a cautionary tale about the dangers of playing god with the course of history. While we may be tempted to use time travel to right past wrongs or prevent future disasters, we must be aware of the potential consequences of our actions. Just as with any new technology, we must exercise caution and responsibility when considering the possibility of time travel.

While time travel is currently impossible, it remains an important subject for ethical speculation. The concept raises a host of difficult questions, from the potential impact on historical authenticity to the question of whether we have the right to change the course of history. As with any new technology, it is important to consider the potential benefits and risks of time travel, and to exercise caution and responsibility when considering its development. While time travel may never become a reality, the ethical questions it raises will continue to be important for scientists, philosophers, and ethicists to consider.

Moreover, there are additional ethical concerns to be considered when it comes to time travel, particularly around the potential impact on individuals and society at large. For example, if time travel were ever to become possible, it is likely that only a select few would have access to the technology, which raises questions about privilege and equity. Who would be allowed to travel through time, and who would be left behind? Would the ability to travel through time be restricted to those with wealth or power, further entrenching existing social inequalities?

Additionally, time travel raises questions about free will and determinism. If the past can be changed, what does that mean for our sense of agency and control over our lives? Would our choices and actions be rendered meaningless if they could be erased or altered at will by someone with access to time travel technology? These questions have implications for our understanding of human nature and our ethical responsibilities to one another.

Another ethical concern related to time travel is the potential for cultural appropriation and erasure. If time travel were possible, there would likely be a strong temptation to revisit historic events or periods in order to experience them firsthand. However, doing so could be seen as a form of cultural appropriation, as travelers would be inserting themselves into a culture or time period that they did not belong to. Additionally, the act of revisiting the past could potentially erase or diminish the experiences and contributions of those who actually lived through those times.

In order to avoid these ethical pitfalls, it is important to approach time travel with a sense of humility and respect for the past. If time travel were ever to become a reality, it would be crucial to approach it in a responsible and thoughtful way, with an eye towards minimizing harm and maximizing benefit. This might involve developing guidelines or ethical codes for time travel, similar to the way that medical professionals have ethical codes to guide their practice.

Ultimately, the ethical considerations surrounding time travel are complex and multifaceted. While the concept remains firmly in the realm of science fiction for now, it is important to continue considering the ethical implications of new technologies and scientific advancements. By doing so, we can ensure that we are using science and technology in a way that benefits humanity as a whole, rather than just a select few. Time travel may never become a reality, but the questions it raises will continue to be relevant for years to come.

Time travel has been a popular concept in science fiction for decades, from H.G. Wells' The Time Machine to Christopher Nolan's Interstellar. The idea of traveling through time and witnessing historical events firsthand is an exciting prospect. However, the concept raises a host of ethical considerations that must be explored.

Imagine if someone traveled back in time and prevented the assassination of President John F. Kennedy. While it may have prevented a tragedy, it would also alter the course of history and potentially lead to a vastly different present-day reality. The question then arises: which reality is more authentic?

For instance, if someone went back in time and prevented the sinking of the Titanic, the passengers who perished on the ship would still exist in the original timeline. However, in the altered timeline, they may never have been born, leading to a completely different set of individuals existing in their place. This raises questions of identity and whether it is ethical to erase someone's existence for the sake of changing history.

For example, If someone traveled back in time and killed their own grandfather, they would create a paradox known as the grandfather paradox. If their grandfather never existed, then they would not exist, making it impossible for them to travel back in time to commit the murder. This creates a loop that defies the laws of causality and makes it difficult to assign blame.

Despite the many ethical considerations, there are also potential benefits to time travel. For example, it could allow us to witness historical events firsthand or help us to better understand the evolution of our species. However, these benefits must be weighed against the potential risks and consequences of meddling with the natural order of time and space.

If we were able to witness historical events firsthand, it could provide a more accurate understanding of what actually happened. For example, if we could go back in time and witness the extinction of the dinosaurs, we could gather valuable information about how it happened and potentially prevent similar events in the future.

Moreover, time travel could also allow us to better understand the evolution of our species. By traveling back in time to observe the lives of our ancestors, we could gain insights into how we evolved and what factors contributed to our development as a species.

However, these benefits must be weighed against the potential risks and consequences of meddling with the natural order of time and space. For instance, if we were to alter the course of history, we may unwittingly create new problems that we are not equipped to handle. Moreover, we may inadvertently create new dangers that we never imagined existed.

Overall, the ethics of time travel is a complex and multifaceted topic that requires careful consideration and examination. As we continue to explore the possibilities of time travel, it is important that we do so with a thoughtful and ethical approach that takes into account the potential impact on the past, present, and future. While time travel may remain firmly in the realm of science fiction, it is not entirely implausible that one day we may discover a way to travel through time. Therefore, it is important that we begin to consider the ethical implications now, rather than waiting until it becomes a reality.

Another ethical concern related to time travel is the concept of free will. If we were able to travel back in time and change the course of events, would we be violating the free will of those who lived in the past? Would we be depriving them of the opportunity to make their own decisions and live their lives as they saw fit?

For example, if we traveled back in time and prevented the American Civil War from happening, we may believe that we are creating a better future. However, we are also denying the individuals who fought and died in that war the opportunity to fight for what they believed in and shape their own destiny.

Moreover, the potential impact of time travel on the environment and the natural world must also be considered. If we were to alter the course of history, we may inadvertently cause irreparable harm to the natural world. For instance, if we prevented a natural disaster from happening in the past, it may have unintended consequences on the environment and the ecosystems that depend on it.

Furthermore, the potential impact of time travel on society and culture must also be taken into account. If we were to change the past, it could have a significant impact on the cultural traditions and social norms of the present day. For example, if we prevented the outbreak of a deadly disease in the past, it may have unintended consequences on the way that society functions and the cultural traditions that have developed as a result of that disease.

In addition, the implications of time travel on personal relationships and identity must also be considered. If we were to travel back in time and interact with our ancestors, it could fundamentally alter our understanding of our own identity and place in the world. Furthermore, if we were to alter the course of our own personal history, it may have unintended consequences on the relationships that we have developed in the present day.

The issue of responsibility is also a significant ethical consideration when it comes to time travel. If someone were to travel back in time and change the course of history, who would be responsible for the consequences of those actions? Would it be the individual who traveled back in time, or would it be society as a whole?

Furthermore, the implications of time travel on the concept of justice must also be explored. If someone were to commit a crime in the past, it may be difficult to hold them accountable in the present day. Moreover, if someone were to travel back in time and prevent a crime from happening, it may be difficult to determine whether or not justice has truly been served.

In conclusion, the ethical considerations surrounding time travel are complex and multifaceted. While the concept remains firmly in the realm of science fiction, it is important that we begin to consider the potential implications now, before it becomes a reality. The impact of time travel on historical authenticity, future generations, accountability, free will, the environment, society and culture, personal relationships and identity, and justice must all be taken into account. Ultimately, any decision regarding time travel must be made with a thoughtful and ethical approach that considers the potential impact on the past, present, and future.

One of the most pressing ethical considerations surrounding time travel is the issue of paradoxes. A paradox is a situation in which a time traveler causes an event that prevents them from ever traveling back in time in the first place. For example, if a time traveler were to go back in time and kill their grandfather before they had children, the time traveler would never be born, which would mean that they could not have traveled back in time to kill their grandfather in the first place. This creates a paradoxical situation that is difficult to resolve.

Moreover, the implications of time travel on scientific progress must also be taken into account. If time travel were possible, it could fundamentally alter the way that science is conducted. For example, scientists could travel back in time to observe historical events or witness the evolution of our planet. This could provide valuable insights into the workings of the natural world and help us to better understand our place in it.

However, the potential benefits of time travel must be weighed against the potential risks and consequences of meddling with the natural order of time and space. Time travel could have unintended consequences that we cannot even imagine, and it is important that we proceed with caution.

Another ethical consideration related to time travel is the impact on personal privacy. If we were able to travel back in time and observe the actions of our ancestors, it could fundamentally alter our understanding of their lives and relationships. This could also have unintended consequences on our own personal relationships and identity.

Furthermore, the impact of time travel on global politics must also be considered. If we were able to travel back in time and alter the course of historical events, it could have significant geopolitical consequences. For example, if we prevented the outbreak of a war in the past, it may fundamentally alter the balance of power in the present day.

The ethical implications of time travel are far-reaching and complex. However, it is important that we continue to explore the possibilities of time travel and consider the ethical considerations that come with it. The future of our species may depend on our ability to make wise and thoughtful decisions about the use of time travel.

Ultimately, any decision regarding time travel must be made with a thoughtful and ethical approach that takes into account the potential impact on the past, present, and future. It is important that we proceed with caution and consider the potential consequences of our actions. The implications of time travel are significant, and we must work together as a global community to ensure that we make the best possible decisions for our planet and our species.

.

## 4. Problem-Solving through Time Travel

Time travel has long been a popular concept in science fiction, with characters using it to solve all manner of problems and overcome obstacles. But could time travel be used in real life to solve some of the world's biggest problems?

One potential application of time travel is in the field of environmental conservation. By traveling back in time and observing the natural world as it existed before human intervention, we could gain valuable insights into how to restore damaged ecosystems and protect vulnerable species.

Time travel could also be used to prevent disasters and tragedies before they occur. By going back in time and warning people of impending danger or taking preventative measures, we could potentially save countless lives and prevent catastrophic events.

Another area where time travel could be useful is in scientific research. By observing historical events and experiments firsthand, we could gain a better understanding of scientific principles and make breakthroughs that might otherwise be impossible.

Of course, there are also potential dangers and risks associated with using time travel to solve problems. The potential impact on the natural order of time and space must be carefully considered, and ethical concerns must be taken into account.

Despite these challenges, the possibilities of using time travel to solve problems are intriguing and warrant further exploration. By unlocking the secrets of time, we may be able to find new solutions to the challenges facing our world.

Time travel has been a topic of fascination for humans since the dawn of time. From ancient myths and legends to modern-day science fiction, the concept of time travel has captured our imaginations and allowed us to explore the infinite possibilities of what the future could hold. But what if time travel could be used in real life to solve some of the world's biggest problems? In this article, we will explore the potential applications of time travel and how it could be used to solve some of the world's most pressing issues.

One potential use of time travel is in the field of environmental conservation. By traveling back in time and observing the natural world as it existed before human intervention, we could gain valuable insights into how to restore damaged ecosystems and protect vulnerable species. Imagine being able to witness the vast herds of bison that once roamed the American plains, or the lush forests that covered the Amazon before it was cleared for agriculture. By studying these past environments, we could learn how to restore them to their former glory and prevent further damage from occurring.

Of course, there are potential dangers associated with this type of time travel. It's possible that by altering the past, we could unintentionally cause even more damage to the environment. Additionally, the impact on the natural order of time and space must be carefully considered, as even small changes to the past could have far-reaching consequences for the present and future.

Another potential application of time travel is in disaster prevention. By going back in time and warning people of impending danger or taking preventative measures, we could potentially save countless lives and prevent catastrophic events. Imagine being able to travel back to 1912 and warn the crew of the Titanic about the iceberg ahead, or being able to stop the 9/11 attacks before they occurred. While this may seem like an unrealistic fantasy, it's important to remember that even small actions in the past could have a significant impact on the future.

However, there are also potential risks associated with using time travel to prevent disasters. It's possible that by altering the past, we could inadvertently cause different disasters to occur, or create unintended consequences that we cannot predict. Additionally, there are ethical concerns to consider when it comes to altering the past, as the rights and freedoms of individuals in the past must be respected.

Another area where time travel could be useful is in scientific research. By observing historical events and experiments firsthand, we could gain a better understanding of scientific principles and make breakthroughs that might otherwise be impossible. Imagine being able to witness the experiments of Galileo, or observe the first flight of the Wright brothers. By studying these past events, we could gain a better understanding of the scientific principles that govern our world and make significant advancements in fields such as physics, engineering, and medicine.

However, there are potential dangers associated with this type of time travel as well. It's possible that by altering the past, we could unintentionally change the course of history and create unintended consequences that we cannot predict. Additionally, there are ethical concerns to consider when it comes to observing historical events, as the privacy and rights of individuals in the past must be respected.

It's important to note that while time travel may seem like a far-off fantasy, there are already theories and technologies that suggest it could be possible in the future. For example, some scientists believe that time travel could be achieved through the use of black holes or wormholes, while others suggest that it could be possible to create a machine that could manipulate time.

One potential application of time travel is in the field of environmental conservation. By traveling back in time and observing the natural world as it existed before human intervention, we could gain valuable insights into how to restore damaged ecosystems and protect vulnerable species. With the increasing threat of climate change, this could be an invaluable tool in the fight to preserve our planet's biodiversity. We could learn from past mistakes and avoid repeating them in the future. For example, we could travel back to the time before industrialization and observe the natural cycles of the environment. This could help us understand how ecosystems functioned before human intervention and how we can help restore them to their former state.

Another application of time travel is in disaster prevention. By going back in time and warning people of impending danger or taking preventative measures, we could potentially save countless lives and prevent catastrophic events. For example, we could travel back to the time before natural disasters such as hurricanes, earthquakes, or tsunamis, and warn people of the impending danger. This could give people the time they need to evacuate and take necessary precautions, potentially saving thousands of lives. Furthermore, we could also use time travel to prevent man-made disasters such as nuclear accidents or terrorist attacks.

Time travel could also be useful in scientific research. By observing historical events and experiments firsthand, we could gain a better understanding of scientific principles and make breakthroughs that might otherwise be impossible. For example, we could travel back to the time of Newton and observe his experiments on gravity. This could help us understand his thought process and provide insights into the principles of physics. Moreover, we could observe historical events such as the discovery of penicillin or the development of the first computer. By doing so, we could learn more about the scientific process and potentially make new discoveries.

Despite the potential benefits of time travel, there are also potential dangers and risks associated with it. One major concern is the potential impact on the natural order of time and space. Altering events in the past could have significant and unforeseen consequences in the present and future. For example, traveling back in time and preventing a disaster may seem like a good idea, but the unintended consequences could be catastrophic. Furthermore, the butterfly effect suggests that even small changes in the past could have significant impacts on the future.

Another concern is the ethical implications of time travel. For example, traveling back in time and changing the course of history could be seen as tampering with free will. It could also raise questions about who has the authority to make decisions about the past and the present. Furthermore, there is the possibility that time travel could be used for personal gain or profit, which could lead to significant ethical concerns.

Despite these challenges, the possibilities of using time travel to solve problems are intriguing and warrant further exploration. By unlocking the secrets of time, we may be able to find new solutions to the challenges facing our world. However, we must proceed with caution and carefully consider the potential risks and ethical implications. Time travel is a fascinating concept, but we must remember that it is still only a concept. We have yet to discover if time travel is possible, let alone develop the technology to make it a reality.

Time travel has the potential to be a powerful tool in solving some of the world's biggest problems. It could be used to restore damaged ecosystems, prevent disasters, and advance scientific research. However, we must also consider the potential risks and ethical implications associated with time travel. Altering events in the past could have significant consequences in the present and future. Therefore, if time travel were to become a reality, we must have a clear understanding of how it works and how to use it responsibly.

One potential way to mitigate the risks associated with time travel is to create guidelines or regulations for its use. This could include limiting the use of time travel to certain circumstances or situations, such as environmental restoration or disaster prevention. It could also involve creating a governing body or agency to oversee time travel and ensure that it is used responsibly and ethically. The development of time travel technology would need to be accompanied by a clear set of rules and protocols to ensure that it is not used for personal gain or other unethical purposes.

Another potential way to mitigate the risks of time travel is to conduct extensive simulations or experiments before attempting to travel through time. By simulating the effects of time travel, we can better understand the potential consequences of altering events in the past. This could help us identify and mitigate potential risks before we attempt to travel through time.

Moreover, we could also consider the implications of time travel for the study of history. Time travel could potentially provide a unique opportunity to experience history firsthand, but it could also change our understanding of the past. For example, what if we were to travel back in time and discover that a historical event we thought we understood was actually quite different from what we had believed? This could raise questions about the reliability of historical records and the nature of historical truth.

Another interesting question is how time travel could impact our understanding of the future. If we were to travel forward in time, would we be able to see the consequences of our actions and make better decisions in the present? Alternatively, could our knowledge of the future lead to unintended consequences or cause us to become complacent in our efforts to solve problems?

Time travel is a fascinating concept with significant potential for solving some of the world's biggest problems. It could be used to restore damaged ecosystems, prevent disasters, and advance scientific research. However, we must also carefully consider the potential risks and ethical implications associated with time travel. If time travel were to become a reality, it would need to be governed by clear rules and protocols to ensure that it is used responsibly and ethically. Furthermore, we must consider the impact of time travel on our understanding of history and the future. As we continue to explore the possibilities of time travel, we must proceed with caution and thoughtful consideration.

One possible way to approach the ethical considerations of time travel is to consider the impact on individuals and societies. If time travel were available only to a select few, it could exacerbate existing social inequalities and create new forms of privilege and disadvantage. Therefore, it is important to ensure that any technology or capability developed is accessible to all and used for the benefit of humanity as a whole.

Another important consideration is the potential impact on personal identity and autonomy. If we could travel back in time and change our past actions, how would this impact our sense of self and our ability to make decisions in the present? Furthermore, if we could travel to the future and see the outcome of our actions, would this affect our ability to make choices and take responsibility for our lives?

There is also the question of how time travel would impact our understanding of cause and effect. If we were able to change events in the past, it would fundamentally alter the course of history and raise questions about the nature of causality. Would events in the present and future be affected by changes made in the past? If so, how would this impact our ability to understand and predict the consequences of our actions?

Despite these challenges, the potential benefits of time travel are significant. In addition to solving environmental and scientific problems, time travel could also be used for personal growth and self-improvement. For example, by traveling back in time and observing our own past behaviors, we could gain insight into our strengths and weaknesses and make positive changes in our lives.

In the field of education, time travel could be used to enhance learning and understanding. By experiencing historical events firsthand, students could gain a deeper appreciation for the complexity and nuance of history. They could also develop critical thinking and problem-solving skills by considering the potential consequences of altering events in the past.

Furthermore, time travel could have significant implications for space exploration and colonization. If we were able to travel through time and space, it could open up new possibilities for exploring and settling other planets. By traveling to the future, we could see how the universe will evolve and plan our exploration accordingly.

Time travel is a complex and fascinating concept with significant potential for solving problems and advancing human knowledge. However, it also raises important ethical considerations and challenges our fundamental understanding of causality and personal identity. As we continue to explore the possibilities of time travel, it is important to approach the technology with caution and consideration. Ultimately, any development of time travel must be accompanied by clear guidelines and protocols to ensure that it is used responsibly and for the benefit of all.

Time travel has always been a popular concept in science fiction, with countless books and movies featuring characters using it to solve all manner of problems and overcome obstacles. However, could time travel be used in real life to solve some of the world's biggest problems? From environmental conservation to disaster prevention and scientific research, time travel presents endless possibilities for solving the challenges facing our world. This article delves into the potential applications of time travel and its associated risks and ethical considerations.

Time Travel and environmental conservation is one area where time travel could prove useful. By traveling back in time and observing the natural world as it existed before human intervention, we could gain valuable insights into how to restore damaged ecosystems and protect vulnerable species. This would involve using time travel technology to go back to a time before the effects of climate change, deforestation, and pollution became rampant. By understanding how the environment looked and functioned in its natural state, we could take better steps towards restoring and preserving it.

For instance, time travel could allow us to observe how an ecosystem functioned in a particular period and what species coexisted in it. This information would be valuable in helping ecologists understand how to restore and rebuild ecosystems in the present day. Furthermore, time travel could help identify the source of environmental damage, which is difficult to determine from the present alone. By identifying the root cause of environmental damage, we could prevent further harm and implement measures to reverse the damage.

Time Travel and Disaster Prevention Time travel could also be used in disaster prevention. By going back in time and warning people of impending danger or taking preventative measures, we could potentially save countless lives and prevent catastrophic events. This would involve traveling back to the past and warning people of the danger that is yet to occur. For instance, if we could travel back in time to before the 2004 Indian Ocean earthquake and tsunami, we could potentially save the lives of the over 200,000 people who perished in the disaster.

Moreover, time travel could help prevent man-made disasters like wars and terrorist attacks. By going back in time and altering the course of history, we could prevent events that led to such catastrophic events. This would involve identifying the root cause of a particular event and changing the course of history to prevent it from happening.

Time Travel and Scientific research is another area where time travel could prove useful. By observing historical events and experiments firsthand, we could gain a better understanding of scientific principles and make breakthroughs that might otherwise be impossible. For instance, time travel could help scientists understand how ancient civilizations like the Egyptians built the pyramids or how the Greek mathematician Archimedes discovered the principle of buoyancy.

Time travel could help scientists conduct experiments that are impossible to carry out in the present day. For instance, we could travel back in time to witness the birth of the universe or observe the behavior of subatomic particles during the Big Bang. By doing so, we could gain new insights into the fundamental laws of nature and make groundbreaking scientific discoveries.

The Potential Risks and Ethical Considerations of Time Travel Despite the many possibilities of using time travel to solve problems, there are also potential dangers and risks associated with it. One significant risk is the potential impact on the natural order of time and space. Time travel could create paradoxes or alter the course of history, leading to unpredictable and unintended consequences. Additionally, traveling back in time could create a temporal loop where a person travels back in time to change an event, which leads to the creation of the same event, creating a never-ending loop.

Moreover, ethical considerations must be taken into account when using time travel to solve problems. For instance, altering the course of history could have unintended consequences on future events and potentially impact the lives of people who were not directly involved in the event. Furthermore, the use of time travel technology could create a power dynamic where those with access to it could wield an unfair advantage over others.

There is also the possibility of altering the natural progression of evolution by introducing knowledge or technology from the future to the past. This could have unforeseen consequences, such as disrupting the development of society or causing a butterfly effect that leads to significant changes in the course of history.

Additionally, the use of time travel technology could have negative psychological effects on individuals who travel through time. Witnessing traumatic events or experiencing culture shock from traveling to a vastly different time period could lead to severe emotional distress or trauma.

The potential applications of time travel to solve problems are intriguing and warrant further exploration. However, it is essential to weigh the benefits against the potential risks and ethical considerations associated with the use of time travel technology. We must ensure that we do not disrupt the natural order of time and space or introduce knowledge or technology that could have unforeseen consequences on the course of history.

Despite the potential dangers, time travel remains an exciting possibility that could revolutionize the way we approach problem-solving in various fields. By unlocking the secrets of time, we may be able to find new solutions to the challenges facing our world, from environmental conservation to disaster prevention and scientific research.

As technology advances, we may one day unlock the secrets of time travel and usher in a new era of problem-solving. However, until then, we must continue to explore the possibilities of time travel while remaining mindful of its associated risks and ethical considerations. Only then can we use this exciting technology to its full potential and make a positive impact on our world.

It is important to note that time travel technology is currently beyond our reach, and there is no guarantee that we will ever develop it. However, the concept of time travel remains a fascinating subject of study for scientists and science fiction writers alike.

In recent years, scientists have made significant strides in the field of quantum mechanics, which could provide new insights into the nature of time and the possibility of time travel. For example, the concept of quantum entanglement, where two particles are connected in such a way that the state of one particle affects the state of the other, could potentially be used to send information back in time.

However, this theory remains highly speculative and is still being explored by scientists. Many experts believe that the development of time travel technology is unlikely, and the risks associated with it outweigh the potential benefits.

In the meantime, science fiction writers continue to explore the possibilities of time travel in their works. From H.G.

Wells' "The Time Machine" to modern-day classics like "Back to the Future" and "Doctor Who," time travel has captured the imaginations of people for generations.

In conclusion, time travel remains a fascinating subject of study and a popular concept in science fiction. While the development of time travel technology is currently beyond our reach, the potential applications of time travel to solve real-world problems are intriguing and warrant further exploration.

However, we must remain mindful of the potential dangers and ethical considerations associated with the use of time travel technology. Only by carefully weighing the benefits against the risks can we use this exciting technology to its full potential and make a positive impact on our world.

As we continue to explore the possibilities of time travel, it is important to remember that our actions have consequences. Altering the course of history or disrupting the natural order of time and space could have severe consequences that we may not be able to anticipate or control.

Therefore, it is essential to approach the development of time travel technology with caution and careful consideration. Any advancements in this field must be made with strict adherence to ethical guidelines and a clear understanding of the potential risks and benefits.

One potential avenue for exploring the possibilities of time travel without the associated risks is through the use of virtual reality technology. By recreating historical events and environments in a virtual space, we can gain valuable insights into the past and use that knowledge to inform our decision-making in the present.

Additionally, virtual reality technology could be used to create simulations of future events, allowing us to prepare for potential disasters or make informed decisions based on the likely outcomes of certain actions.

Time travel technology may remain beyond our reach for the foreseeable future, we can still explore the possibilities of time travel through other means, such as virtual reality technology. By carefully considering the potential risks and benefits of time travel, we can make informed decisions about how to use this exciting technology to solve real-world problems and make a positive impact on our world.

.

# 5.  Unraveling the Science of Time Travel

The theory of relativity, proposed by Albert Einstein in the early 20th century, revolutionized our understanding of space and time. According to this theory, time is not absolute but is relative to the observer and the speed at which they are traveling.

One of the implications of relativity is the phenomenon of time dilation, where time appears to move slower for objects that are moving at high speeds relative to stationary objects. This effect has been confirmed through experiments and is a key factor in the potential for time travel.

Another implication of relativity for time travel is the concept of wormholes. These are theoretical tunnels through spacetime that could potentially allow for faster-than-light travel and time travel. However, the existence of wormholes remains purely hypothetical at this point.

While the concept of time travel remains firmly in the realm of science fiction, the theory of relativity has provided valuable insights into the nature of time and its relationship with space and matter. By continuing to explore the implications of relativity, we may one day be able to unlock the secrets of time travel and explore the unseen possibilities of the universe.

The theory of relativity, proposed by Albert Einstein in the early 20th century, revolutionized our understanding of space and time. Einstein's theory was based on the observation that the laws of physics appear to be the same for all observers moving at a constant speed relative to one another. This principle is known as the principle of relativity.

Time dilation is a complicated concept that requires a basic understanding of Einstein's theory of relativity. It states that as an object's velocity increases, time slows down for that object relative to an observer who is stationary. This effect is only noticeable when an object is traveling at extremely high speeds, close to the speed of light. At this point, the difference in the rate of time between the moving object and the stationary object becomes significant. For example, if a spacecraft were to travel at close to the speed of light for a year, time would have slowed down for the astronauts inside the spacecraft. When they returned to Earth, they would have aged less than their counterparts who remained on Earth.

The concept of time dilation has been confirmed through experiments. The most famous of these is the Hafele-Keating experiment, which was conducted in 1971. This experiment involved placing atomic clocks on commercial airliners and then flying them around the world in opposite directions. The clocks on the planes were compared to stationary clocks on the ground, and the results confirmed that time dilation was occurring. The planes had aged less than the clocks on the ground.

The concept of time dilation has important implications for the potential for time travel. If time can be slowed down or sped up for an object relative to a stationary observer, then it may be possible to travel through time. For example, if a spacecraft were to travel at close to the speed of light for a certain period, then the astronauts on board could potentially travel forward in time. When they returned to Earth, they would find that more time had passed than they had experienced. This concept of time travel is a staple of science fiction, but it has a basis in scientific fact.

Another concept that has important implications for time travel is the concept of wormholes. A wormhole is a hypothetical tunnel through spacetime that could potentially allow for faster-than-light travel and time travel. According to the theory of relativity, wormholes are possible, but they remain purely hypothetical at this point. Wormholes are a complex concept that requires a deep understanding of physics, but the basic idea is that they could be used to travel great distances in space or even travel through time.

The concept of wormholes is fascinating because it suggests that it may be possible to travel through time without actually having to travel at extremely high speeds. Instead, a wormhole could be used to create a shortcut through spacetime, allowing an object to travel vast distances in space or even travel through time. However, the existence of wormholes remains purely hypothetical, and there is no evidence to suggest that they actually exist.

While the concept of time travel remains firmly in the realm of science fiction, the theory of relativity has provided valuable insights into the nature of time and its relationship with space and matter. By continuing to explore the implications of relativity, we may one day be able to unlock the secrets of time travel and explore the unseen possibilities of the universe.

The theory of relativity has had a profound impact on our understanding of the universe. It has challenged our preconceived notions of space and time, and it has opened up a new realm of possibilities for scientific exploration. It has also led to the development of new technologies, such as GPS systems, which rely on the principles of relativity to function accurately.

One of the most significant impacts of relativity has been on our understanding of the nature of space and time. Before Einstein's theories, space and time were viewed as two separate and distinct concepts. However, relativity showed that they are inextricably linked and that the fabric of spacetime is affected by the presence of matter and energy. This idea has revolutionized our understanding of gravity and has led to the development of new theories, such as string theory, which attempt to explain the nature of the universe at a fundamental level.

The concept of time dilation has also led to new developments in science and technology. For example, it has been used to develop the idea of time capsules, which are designed to preserve important artifacts for future generations. By using time dilation, it is possible to slow down time for these artifacts, which means that they can be preserved for much longer periods than would otherwise be possible.

The concept of wormholes has also captured the imagination of scientists and the public alike. While the existence of wormholes remains purely hypothetical, scientists are actively searching for evidence that they may exist. Some physicists believe that the Large Hadron Collider (LHC) could be used to create wormholes, although this remains a topic of debate within the scientific community.

Another area where the theory of relativity has had a significant impact is in the development of our understanding of black holes. Black holes are incredibly dense objects that are formed when a massive star collapses in on itself. According to relativity, the gravitational force around a black hole is so strong that nothing can escape from it, not even light. This has led to the development of new theories, such as Hawking radiation, which attempt to explain the behavior of black holes.

The study of black holes has also led to the development of the concept of a singularity, which is a point of infinite density at the center of a black hole. According to relativity, the laws of physics break down at a singularity, which means that we cannot use our current understanding of the universe to explain what happens inside a black hole. This has led to the development of new theories, such as loop quantum gravity, which attempt to explain the behavior of black holes at a fundamental level.

The theory of relativity has also had a significant impact on the development of modern cosmology. Cosmology is the study of the universe as a whole, and it attempts to answer some of the most fundamental questions about our existence, such as how the universe began and what its ultimate fate will be. Relativity has provided the foundation for modern cosmology, and it has led to the development of new theories, such as inflationary cosmology, which attempt to explain the behavior of the universe in its earliest moments.

Despite the profound impact that relativity has had on our understanding of the universe, there is still much that we do not know. For example, we still do not know what dark matter and dark energy are, although they are believed to make up the majority of the mass-energy in the universe. We also do not know how to reconcile relativity with quantum mechanics, which is the other fundamental theory of physics.

One of the most significant implications of relativity is the phenomenon of time dilation. According to relativity, time is not absolute but is relative to the observer and the speed at which they are traveling. As objects approach the speed of light, time appears to slow down, which means that objects moving at high speeds relative to stationary objects will experience time differently. This effect has been confirmed through experiments and is a key factor in the potential for time travel.

Time dilation has been observed in various experiments. For example, scientists have measured the decay of subatomic particles traveling at high speeds and found that they appear to live longer than those at rest. This phenomenon has been observed in particle accelerators, where subatomic particles are accelerated to close to the speed of light.

The concept of time dilation has significant implications for space travel. If astronauts were to travel at high speeds relative to the Earth, they would experience time differently than people on Earth. This means that if they were to return to Earth after a long journey, they would have aged less than their counterparts on Earth. This effect is known as the twin paradox.

Another implication of relativity for time travel is the concept of wormholes. These are theoretical tunnels through spacetime that could potentially allow for faster-than-light travel and time travel. However, the existence of wormholes remains purely hypothetical at this point. Wormholes are predicted by the equations of general relativity but have never been observed.

The concept of wormholes has captured the imagination of science fiction writers and scientists alike. If wormholes do exist, they could provide a shortcut through spacetime, allowing for travel between distant points in the universe. This could potentially allow us to travel through time as well, by traveling through a wormhole that leads to a different point in time.

One of the challenges of exploring the possibility of time travel is the issue of causality. According to relativity, events are related to one another in a cause-and-effect chain. If time travel were possible, it could potentially create paradoxes where cause and effect are reversed or violated. This issue is known as the grandfather paradox, where a time traveler could potentially travel back in time and prevent their grandparents from meeting, which would mean that the time traveler would never have been born.

Another implication of relativity is the concept of spacetime, which unifies space and time into a single four-dimensional continuum. According to relativity, time and space are not separate entities but are two aspects of the same thing. This means that events that appear to occur at different times and in different places are actually part of a single spacetime event.

The concept of spacetime has led to the idea of curved spacetime, where the presence of matter and energy can warp the fabric of spacetime. This warping effect is what we experience as gravity. The concept of curved spacetime has been confirmed through experiments, such as the observation of the bending of light around massive objects like stars.

The theory of relativity has also led to the concept of black holes, which are regions of spacetime where gravity is so strong that nothing, not even light, can escape.

The idea of black holes was initially met with skepticism but has since been confirmed through various observations. For example, astronomers have observed stars orbiting around a point in space where there appears to be no visible object. This point is known as a black hole, and it is believed to be the result of the collapse of a massive star.

The concept of black holes has significant implications for our understanding of the universe. Black holes are thought to play a critical role in the evolution of galaxies, as they can influence the motion of stars and other objects in their vicinity. The study of black holes has also led to the development of new areas of physics, such as black hole thermodynamics and the holographic principle.

The holographic principle is based on the idea that the information contained in a region of space can be encoded on the boundary of that region. This principle has significant implications for our understanding of the universe, as it suggests that the information contained within a black hole can be encoded on its event horizon, the boundary beyond which nothing can escape.

The study of black holes has also led to the development of the theory of quantum gravity, which aims to unify quantum mechanics and general relativity. Quantum mechanics is the study of the behavior of particles on a small scale, while general relativity describes the behavior of objects on a large scale. The unification of these two theories is one of the most significant challenges in modern physics.

The study of black holes and other objects in the universe has also led to the discovery of dark matter and dark energy. Dark matter is thought to make up the majority of the matter in the universe, but it cannot be observed directly as it does not emit, absorb or reflect light. Dark energy, on the other hand, is a mysterious force that is causing the expansion of the universe to accelerate.

The discovery of dark matter and dark energy has significant implications for our understanding of the universe. The existence of dark matter helps to explain the observed gravitational effects on objects in the universe, while dark energy is thought to be responsible for the observed acceleration of the expansion of the universe.

The study of relativity has also led to the development of new technologies, such as the global positioning system (GPS). GPS relies on the principles of relativity to accurately determine the position of objects on Earth. The satellites that make up the GPS system are equipped with atomic clocks that are synchronized with clocks on the ground. The clocks on the satellites run slightly slower than the clocks on the ground due to the effects of time dilation, which allows for the accurate determination of position.

The theory of relativity has had a profound impact on our understanding of space and time. The concepts of time dilation, curved spacetime, black holes, and the unification of quantum mechanics and general relativity have led to new insights into the nature of the universe. While the concept of time travel remains firmly in the realm of science fiction, the study of relativity has provided valuable insights into the nature of time and its relationship with space and matter. As we continue to explore the implications of relativity and other areas of physics, we may one day be able to unlock the secrets of time travel and explore the unseen possibilities of the universe.

The study of relativity has also provided insights into the nature of the early universe. According to the theory of relativity, the universe began as a singularity, a point of infinite density and temperature. This singularity then underwent a period of rapid expansion known as inflation, which is thought to have lasted for a fraction of a second. This expansion is thought to have smoothed out the distribution of matter and energy in the universe, leading to the formation of galaxies and other structures.

The study of the early universe has also led to the development of the theory of cosmic inflation, which proposes that the universe underwent a period of exponential expansion shortly after the Big Bang. This theory helps to explain a number of observed features of the universe, such as its large-scale homogeneity and isotropy, as well as the lack of observed magnetic monopoles.

The study of relativity and other areas of physics has also led to the development of new technologies, such as particle accelerators and telescopes. Particle accelerators are used to study the behavior of particles at high energies, which can help to shed light on the fundamental nature of matter and energy. Telescopes, on the other hand, allow us to observe objects in the universe that are too distant to be seen with the naked eye.

One of the most significant challenges in modern physics is the unification of the four fundamental forces of nature: gravity, electromagnetism, and the strong and weak nuclear forces. The study of relativity and other areas of physics has led to the development of theories such as string theory, which proposes that the fundamental building blocks of the universe are not particles but tiny, one-dimensional strings.

While string theory remains a highly speculative area of physics, it has the potential to provide a unified description of the fundamental forces of nature. It is also one of the few theories that incorporates the principles of both quantum mechanics and general relativity, which makes it a promising avenue for the unification of these two theories.

The theory of relativity has had a profound impact on our understanding of the universe. It has led to new insights into the nature of time, space, and matter, as well as the development of new technologies and the discovery of new phenomena such as black holes and dark matter. As we continue to explore the implications of relativity and other areas of physics, we may one day be able to unlock the secrets of the universe and understand the fundamental nature of the cosmos.

According to the theory of relativity, time is not absolute. Instead, time is relative to the observer and the speed at which they are traveling. This idea may sound strange at first, but it has been confirmed through countless experiments and observations.

Time dilation may seem like a minor phenomenon, but it has important implications for the concept of time travel. The idea of time travel has long been a popular topic in science fiction, but could it really be possible? The concept of time dilation suggests that it may be possible to travel forward in time, at least in theory.

Imagine that you are on a spaceship traveling at near-light speed. According to the theory of relativity, time will appear to move more slowly for you than it would for someone on

Earth. If you were to return to Earth after a long journey, you would have experienced less time than someone who stayed on Earth. In other words, you will have traveled into the future.

While traveling into the future may be possible, traveling into the past is a much more complicated proposition. However, the theory of relativity does provide some possible avenues for time travel to the past.

Despite the many unknowns surrounding the concept of time travel, the theory of relativity has provided valuable insights into the nature of time and its relationship with space and matter. By continuing to explore the implications of relativity, scientists may one day be able to unlock the secrets of time travel and explore the unseen possibilities of the universe.

One of the most important aspects of relativity is its impact on our understanding of space. According to the theory of relativity, space is not static and unchanging. Instead, space is influenced by matter and energy, and it can be warped and distorted.

This idea is perhaps best illustrated by the concept of gravitational lensing. Gravitational lensing occurs when a massive object, such as a galaxy or a black hole, bends the path of light around it. This phenomenon is a direct result of the warping of space caused by the massive object.

The space-time continuum has important implications for our understanding of the universe. It suggests that the fabric of space and time is not fixed, but is instead constantly changing and evolving. This idea has been confirmed by observations of the universe, such as the discovery of dark energy, which is thought to be responsible for the accelerating expansion of the universe.

The concept of the space-time continuum also has implications for our understanding of the fundamental nature of reality. According to relativity, there is no single, objective reality that exists independently of the observer. Instead, reality is relative and depends on the observer's position and velocity.

This idea is often illustrated by the famous "twin paradox." In this thought experiment, one twin stays on Earth while the other twin travels through space at high speeds. When the traveling twin returns to Earth, they will have experienced less time than the twin who stayed on Earth, as a result of time dilation. From the perspective of the traveling twin, they have aged less than their twin on Earth. This paradox demonstrates the relative nature of time and the importance of the observer's perspective.

The implications of relativity are not limited to the field of physics. The concept of relativity has had a profound impact on our understanding of philosophy, culture, and even art. The idea that there is no objective reality has challenged our traditional views of truth and has led to a greater appreciation for diversity and subjectivity.

In the world of art, the concept of relativity has inspired new forms of expression, such as cubism, which sought to depict multiple perspectives simultaneously. The influence of relativity can also be seen in the works of modern artists, such as Salvador Dali and MC Escher, who explored the nature of perception and reality in their art.

Despite the many implications of relativity, there are still many unanswered questions about the nature of space and time. For example, the theory of relativity is incompatible with quantum mechanics, the branch of physics that deals with the behavior of matter and energy on a very small scale.

Scientists are currently working to develop a theory that can reconcile these two seemingly incompatible theories. The search for a "theory of everything" is one of the greatest challenges facing modern physics, and it is hoped that such a theory will provide a complete understanding of the fundamental nature of reality.

In conclusion, the theory of relativity has had a profound impact on our understanding of space and time. The idea that time is relative and that space can be warped has challenged our traditional views of the universe and has inspired new forms of expression in art and culture.

Furthermore, the theory of relativity has also led to technological advancements in fields such as GPS navigation. GPS works by measuring the time it takes for signals to travel from satellites to receivers on Earth. However, because the satellites are in motion and experience time dilation, their clocks run at a slightly different rate than clocks on Earth. Without taking into account the effects of relativity, GPS measurements would be inaccurate by several kilometers.

The impact of relativity is not limited to technology and art but also extends to our understanding of the universe itself. The concept of wormholes, which is based on the theory of relativity, could potentially provide a way to travel faster than the speed of light and even travel back in time.

However, the existence of wormholes remains purely theoretical at this point. The intense gravitational forces required to create a wormhole would likely require a source of negative energy or exotic matter, which is currently beyond our technological capabilities to produce or harness.

Despite the challenges of exploring the possibilities of wormholes, the implications of relativity continue to inspire new avenues of research and exploration. Scientists continue to explore the nature of space and time and work towards a deeper understanding of the universe and its fundamental laws.

The study of relativity has also led to a greater appreciation for the role of mathematics in the natural sciences. The equations used to describe the phenomena of relativity are some of the most complex and beautiful in all of physics. The use of mathematical models to describe the behavior of the universe has become an essential tool in modern physics and has allowed scientists to make predictions about the behavior of matter and energy that have been confirmed through experiments.

In conclusion, the theory of relativity has had a profound impact on our understanding of the nature of the universe, from the behavior of space and time to the role of mathematics in describing the behavior of matter and energy. While the concept of time travel remains firmly in the realm of science fiction, the implications of relativity continue to inspire new avenues of research and exploration.

As we continue to explore the mysteries of the universe, it is clear that the insights provided by relativity will continue to play a vital role in our understanding of the fundamental nature of reality. From the study of black holes and the behavior of the universe at the largest scales to the development of new technologies and forms of expression, the theory of relativity will continue to shape the way we think about the world around us for many years to come.

.

## 6. Future Technologies

As technology continues to advance at a rapid pace, it is clear that the future holds many exciting possibilities. From space exploration to artificial intelligence, there are countless ways in which technology could transform our lives and reshape our world. One area where technology could have a significant impact is in the field of time travel. While time travel remains firmly in the realm of science fiction, advances in areas such as quantum computing and wormhole research are bringing us closer than ever to unlocking the secrets of time.

In the coming decades, it is likely that we will see significant progress in the development of time travel technology. This could open up new frontiers for exploration and allow us to witness historical events firsthand.

But with these exciting possibilities come significant challenges and risks. The potential impact on the natural order of time and space must be carefully considered, as well as the ethical implications of altering the course of history.

Despite these challenges, it is clear that the future of technology holds many exciting possibilities. By continuing to push the boundaries of what is possible, we may one day be able to explore the unseen possibilities of time and reshape the course of history itself.

As technology continues to advance at an incredible pace, the possibilities for the future are endless. From exploring space to creating artificial intelligence, technology is transforming our lives and reshaping our world. One area where technology could have a significant impact is in the field of time travel. Although it remains in the realm of science fiction, advances in areas such as quantum computing and wormhole research are bringing us closer than ever to unlocking the secrets of time.

Time travel has always been a subject of fascination for people across the world. From movies to books, people have always imagined the possibilities of traveling through time. However, the concept of time travel has been dismissed as a mere fantasy or an impossibility for many years. But with the advancements in technology and research, this concept is no longer a distant dream.

With quantum computing, scientists can now simulate the behavior of particles in the past or the future. This technology is based on the principle of quantum entanglement, which allows two particles to be connected in such a way that the state of one particle affects the state of the other, even if they are separated by a large distance. This technology is being used to simulate the behavior of particles in the past or the future, which could potentially lead to time travel.

Another area where time travel could become possible is wormhole research. A wormhole is a theoretical passage through space-time that could potentially connect two distant points in space and time. While the existence of wormholes is still a topic of debate among scientists, recent research has shown that they could be used to travel through time.

In the coming decades, it is likely that we will see significant progress in the development of time travel technology. This could open up new frontiers for exploration and allow us to witness historical events firsthand. For example, we could travel back in time to witness the signing of the Declaration of Independence or travel to the future to witness the colonization of Mars.

However, with these exciting possibilities come significant challenges and risks. The potential impact on the natural order of time and space must be carefully considered, as well as the ethical implications of altering the course of history. For example, if we were to travel back in time and prevent a historical event from happening, we could potentially alter the course of history and create unforeseen consequences.

Furthermore, time travel could also have a significant impact on the environment. If we were to travel back in time and change something, it could have unintended consequences on the future. This could potentially create a ripple effect that could have disastrous consequences on the environment.

Despite these challenges, it is clear that the future of technology holds many exciting possibilities. By continuing to push the boundaries of what is possible, we may one day be able to explore the unseen possibilities of time and reshape the course of history itself. With the rapid pace of technological advancement, it is only a matter of time before we unlock the secrets of time travel and create a new era of exploration and discovery.

Quantum computing is a field of study that involves harnessing the power of quantum mechanics to perform calculations at lightning-fast speeds. This technology has the potential to revolutionize many areas of science and engineering, including the development of time travel technology.

One of the ways in which quantum computing could be used to enable time travel is through the creation of what are known as "quantum computers." These devices would be able to manipulate the fabric of time and space in such a way as to allow for time travel.

Another area of research that has shown great promise for enabling time travel is wormhole research. Wormholes are hypothetical objects that exist within the fabric of space and time, connecting different points in spacetime.

The idea of using wormholes for time travel is not a new one. In fact, it has been the subject of much speculation among physicists and science fiction writers for decades. However, recent advances in our understanding of the physics of wormholes have brought us closer than ever before to understanding how they might be used for time travel.

Despite the potential for time travel to revolutionize our understanding of the universe, there are significant challenges and risks associated with this technology. One of the most significant challenges is the potential impact on the natural order of time and space.

If time travel were to become a reality, it could have a profound impact on the way we view history and the course of events. For example, if we were able to travel back in time and alter the course of history, it could have far-reaching and unpredictable consequences for the future.

Another major challenge associated with time travel is the ethical implications of altering the course of history. Many people argue that it is not ethical to change the course of events in the past, as it could have a significant impact on the lives of people in the future.

Despite these challenges, the potential benefits of time travel cannot be ignored. For example, it could allow us to witness historical events firsthand and gain a deeper understanding of our place in the universe. It could also open up new frontiers for exploration and discovery, enabling us to travel to distant parts of the universe and explore worlds that were previously beyond our reach.

As we look to the future, it is clear that the development of time travel technology holds great promise. However, it is also clear that we must approach this technology with caution and carefully consider the potential risks and challenges associated with it. By doing so, we can ensure that we use this technology in a responsible and ethical way, and unlock the many exciting possibilities that the future holds.

One of the key challenges associated with developing time travel technology is the question of whether it is even possible. Despite the significant progress that has been made in areas such as quantum computing and wormhole research, there are still many unanswered questions surrounding the physics of time travel.

One of the biggest obstacles to time travel is the so-called "grandfather paradox." This paradox arises when a time traveler goes back in time and prevents their own existence. For example, if a time traveler were to go back in time and kill their grandfather before their own parent was born, then they would never have been born themselves, creating a paradox.

Another challenge associated with time travel is the issue of causality. If we were able to travel back in time and alter the course of history, it could have a ripple effect that would impact the future in unpredictable ways. For example, changing one event in the past could lead to a chain reaction of events that would result in a vastly different future.

Despite these challenges, many researchers remain optimistic about the potential for time travel to revolutionize our understanding of the universe. Some scientists believe that time travel could hold the key to solving some of the greatest mysteries of physics, such as the nature of dark matter and dark energy.

In addition to its scientific potential, time travel also holds significant cultural and historical significance. For example, it could allow us to witness some of the most pivotal moments in human history, such as the signing of the Declaration of Independence or the landing of the first humans on the moon.

However, with great power comes great responsibility. The ethical implications of time travel cannot be ignored. For example, if we were able to travel back in time and prevent some of the greatest tragedies in history, such as the Holocaust or the September 11th attacks, should we do so? And if we did, what unintended consequences might arise as a result?

Ultimately, the development of time travel technology is likely to be a slow and painstaking process. It will require years of research, experimentation, and careful consideration of the potential risks and benefits associated with this technology. However, as our understanding of the physics of time and space continues to evolve, it seems increasingly likely that we will one day be able to unlock the secrets of time and reshape the course of history itself.

One of the most famous theories involving wormholes and time travel is known as the "Einstein-Rosen bridge." This theory suggests that two black holes could be connected by a wormhole, allowing us to travel between them and potentially even travel through time.

Another area of research that could be instrumental in the development of time travel technology is quantum computing. Quantum computing is a field that explores the potential of quantum mechanics to revolutionize the way we process information. Some researchers believe that quantum computing could be the key to unlocking the secrets of time travel, as it could allow us to perform calculations that are currently impossible using classical computing methods.

Despite the potential benefits of time travel technology, there are also significant risks and ethical considerations to be taken into account. For example, altering the course of history could have unintended consequences that could be catastrophic. Furthermore, the possibility of time travel could create a host of legal and moral dilemmas, such as the potential for time travelers to profit from insider knowledge or to commit crimes with no fear of being caught.

In addition, time travel could have a profound impact on our understanding of free will and determinism. If we are able to travel through time and change the course of history, does that mean that our future is predetermined? And if we are able to change the past, what does that mean for our sense of agency and responsibility in the present?

The development of time travel technology is an exciting and complex field that holds significant promise for the future of science and humanity. While there are significant challenges and risks associated with this technology, the potential benefits are enormous. By continuing to push the boundaries of what is possible and remaining mindful of the ethical considerations involved, we may one day be able to explore the unseen possibilities of time and space and revolutionize our understanding of the universe.

As we delve deeper into the possibilities of time travel, it is important to consider the various models and theories that have been proposed to understand the nature of time itself. One popular model is known as the "block universe" or "four-dimensionalism" model. This model suggests that time is not linear, but rather that all events that have ever happened or will happen exist simultaneously in a four-dimensional block.

According to this model, time travel would not necessarily involve "going back" in time, but rather moving through the four-dimensional block to a different point in space-time. However, this model raises questions about free will and determinism, as well as the nature of causality and the potential for paradoxes.

Another model that has been proposed to understand time is known as the "presentism" model. This model suggests that only the present moment exists, and that the past and future are mere abstractions. According to this model, time travel would involve physically moving from one moment in the present to another.

Both of these models have their own strengths and weaknesses, and the debate over the nature of time and the potential for time travel remains a topic of intense discussion and research.

One of the most well-known paradoxes associated with time travel is known as the "grandfather paradox." This paradox suggests that if one were to travel back in time and prevent their grandfather from meeting their grandmother, they would effectively erase their own existence. This paradox highlights the potential for time travel to disrupt the natural order of causality and raises questions about the ethical implications of altering history.

Another paradox associated with time travel is the "bootstrap paradox." This paradox involves a time traveler bringing back an object or idea from the future and introducing it to the past, effectively creating a "loop" in which the object or idea has no clear origin. This paradox raises questions about the nature of causality and the potential for time travel to create infinite regressions.

In addition, time travel could have significant implications for space exploration. For example, if we were able to travel through time and space, we could potentially explore distant galaxies and observe the evolution of the universe firsthand.

While the development of time travel technology may still be many years away, it is clear that the potential benefits and risks of this technology are significant. As we continue to push the boundaries of what is possible, it is important to remain mindful of the ethical considerations and potential consequences of this technology.

In addition to the theoretical and philosophical implications of time travel, there are also many practical considerations to take into account. For example, the development of time travel technology would require significant resources and infrastructure, as well as a rigorous system of regulation and oversight to ensure the safe and responsible use of this technology.

The potential impact of time travel on the environment and natural resources must also be carefully considered. For example, the energy required to power time travel technology could have significant environmental consequences, and the potential for time travelers to inadvertently introduce foreign contaminants to different time periods could have unforeseen ecological impacts.

The development of time travel technology is a complex and exciting field that holds significant promise for the future of science and humanity. While there are significant challenges and risks associated with this technology, the potential benefits are immense, from space exploration to historical research and beyond. As we continue to explore the possibilities of time travel, it is important to remain mindful of the ethical and practical considerations involved, and to work towards a responsible and sustainable approach to this technology.

Despite these challenges, researchers are actively working to better understand the nature of wormholes and to develop the technology necessary to harness their potential. This research involves a combination of theoretical physics, computational modeling, and experimental testing, and progress in this area could have significant implications for the future of space exploration and time travel.

Another area of research that is closely related to time travel is the study of parallel universes. According to some theoretical models, there may exist multiple parallel universes, each with its own unique space-time fabric and history. If this is true, it may be possible to travel between these parallel universes and witness different versions of reality.

While the study of parallel universes is still in its early stages, it holds significant promise for the future of physics and cosmology. By better understanding the nature of the universe and the potential for multiple realities, we may be able to unlock new avenues for exploration and discovery.

Of course, the development of time travel technology raises many ethical and philosophical questions, particularly with regard to the potential impact on the natural order of time and space. One concern is that time travel could lead to the creation of paradoxes or the alteration of historical events, with unforeseeable consequences.

Another concern is the potential for time travel to create inequality and social unrest. If only a select few individuals or groups have access to time travel technology, this could lead to significant disparities in power and influence, with far-reaching social and political implications.

To address these concerns, it will be necessary to establish a rigorous system of regulation and oversight for the development and use of time travel technology. This may involve international agreements and cooperation, as well as the establishment of ethical guidelines and standards for the responsible use of this technology. It will be important to consider the potential impact of time travel on different cultures and societies. For example, the introduction of future technology or ideas to past cultures could have significant cultural and social implications, and it will be important to approach this technology with sensitivity and respect for different perspectives and values.

The development of time travel technology represents a significant frontier in the field of science and technology, with immense potential for the future of humanity. While there are many challenges and risks associated with this technology, the potential benefits are significant, from space exploration to historical research and beyond.

Time travel has always been a fascinating topic in science fiction. However, with advances in areas such as quantum computing and wormhole research, we are getting closer than ever to unlocking the secrets of time. In the coming decades, it is likely that we will see significant progress in the development of time travel technology. This could open up new frontiers for exploration and allow us to witness historical events firsthand.

Another challenge is the ethical implications of altering the course of history. If time travel were to become a reality, who would have the power to use it? Would it be ethical to alter the course of history for personal gain or political purposes? These are important questions that must be carefully considered before time travel technology is developed.

Despite these challenges, there are still many potential benefits to time travel technology. For example, it could allow us to witness historical events firsthand, giving us a better understanding of our past. It could also provide us with new insights into the future, allowing us to better prepare for potential disasters or unforeseen events.

Despite the challenges and risks involved, many scientists believe that time travel technology is within the realm of possibility. With continued research and development, we may one day be able to explore the unseen possibilities of time and reshape the course of history itself.

One of the potential applications of time travel technology is in the field of archaeology. Imagine being able to travel back in time and witness ancient civilizations firsthand, or even interact with them. This could revolutionize our understanding of history and provide us with new insights into the lives and cultures of our ancestors.

In addition to archaeology, time travel could also have significant implications for space exploration. Imagine being able to travel back in time and witness the formation of the universe, or witness the birth of a star. This could provide us with a better understanding of the cosmos and help us unlock the secrets of the universe.

Of course, with the potential benefits of time travel come significant risks and challenges. For example, the mere existence of time travel technology could lead to a breakdown in the natural order of time and space. If time travel were to become widely available, it could lead to chaos and instability as people attempt to alter the past for personal gain or political purposes.

Another challenge is the potential impact on our understanding of free will. If time travel were possible, would our actions in the past be predetermined, or would we have the ability to change the course of history? This is a philosophical question that has yet to be fully explored.

Despite these challenges, many scientists believe that time travel is not only possible but inevitable. As we continue to push the boundaries of what is possible, we may one day be able to unlock the secrets of time and explore the unseen possibilities of the universe.

In order to achieve this, we will need to continue to invest in research and development. This will require significant funding and resources, as well as a global commitment to scientific progress. However, the potential benefits of time travel technology are too great to ignore, and the future of our civilization may depend on our ability to explore the unseen possibilities of time.

As we continue to explore the potential of time travel technology, it is important to consider the ethical implications of altering the course of history. If we are able to travel back in time and witness historical events, should we interfere or simply observe? What if our actions inadvertently alter the course of history in ways we could not have predicted?

These are complex questions with no easy answers, but they are questions that we must confront if we are to fully understand the implications of time travel technology. One possible solution is to establish strict regulations and guidelines for the use of time travel technology, similar to the regulations that currently govern scientific research.

Another potential challenge is the impact of time travel on our understanding of causality. If we are able to travel back in time and alter events, what impact will this have on our understanding of cause and effect? Will it lead to a breakdown in our understanding of the natural order of the universe?

In addition to the scientific and philosophical implications of time travel technology, there are also numerous practical applications that could have significant benefits for humanity. For example, time travel technology could be used to prevent disasters before they happen, or to help people cope with traumatic events by allowing them to revisit past experiences and confront their fears.

Another potential application is in the field of medicine. Time travel technology could allow doctors to observe the progression of diseases in real-time, and to test the effectiveness of potential treatments on patients in the past.

Of course, these potential benefits come with significant risks, including the potential for abuse and the impact on our understanding of free will. However, with careful planning and regulation, the benefits of time travel technology may outweigh the risks.

The development of time travel technology is one of the most exciting possibilities on the horizon of technological advancement. While there are significant challenges and risks involved, the potential benefits are too great to ignore. By continuing to invest in research and development, we may one day be able to explore the unseen possibilities of time and space, and unlock the secrets of the universe. However, this will require a global commitment to scientific progress, a willingness to confront the ethical and philosophical implications of altering the course of history, and a dedication to responsible regulation and oversight.

.

## 7. Time Travel and Multiverse Theories

According to the multiverse theory, every possible outcome of every event exists in a separate universe. This means that if time travel were possible, any changes made to the past would not affect our own universe but would instead create a new parallel universe.

This has significant implications for the potential risks and consequences of time travel. While altering the past in our own universe could have disastrous consequences, it is possible that changes made in a parallel universe could have less severe or even positive outcomes.

As we continue to explore the possibilities of time travel, the concept of the multiverse will likely play an increasingly important role in shaping our understanding of the potential risks and benefits of altering the course of history.

For centuries, humans have been fascinated with the idea of time travel. From H.G. Wells' "The Time Machine" to the iconic "Back to the Future" film franchise, we have explored the concept of traveling through time and altering the course of history. However, the idea of time travel has always been shrouded in mystery and controversy. Is it possible? And if so, what are the implications of changing the past?

One of the most intriguing concepts in modern physics is the idea of the multiverse, a theoretical construct that suggests the existence of an infinite number of parallel universes. This concept has significant implications for the potential of time travel.

According to the multiverse theory, every possible outcome of every event exists in a separate universe. This means that if time travel were possible, any changes made to the past would not affect our own universe but would instead create a new parallel universe. In other words, if you traveled back in time and prevented the assassination of President John F. Kennedy, you would not return to a world where Kennedy survived. Instead, you would find yourself in a new universe where he was never killed, and the course of history had been altered.

This has significant implications for the potential risks and consequences of time travel. While altering the past in our own universe could have disastrous consequences, it is possible that changes made in a parallel universe could have less severe or even positive outcomes. For example, if you traveled back in time and prevented a natural disaster from occurring, you could create a new universe where that disaster never happened, potentially saving countless lives.

Of course, the multiverse theory remains purely hypothetical at this point, and there is no way to confirm its existence or the potential implications for time travel. However, it remains an intriguing possibility that continues to fascinate scientists and science fiction writers alike.

One of the key challenges in exploring the concept of time travel and the multiverse is the nature of causality. In our universe, cause and effect are tightly linked. If you drop a ball, it falls to the ground because of the force of gravity. If you remove the force of gravity, the ball would no longer fall. However, in a multiverse where every possible outcome exists, causality becomes more complex. If you prevent an event from occurring, it may not have the same impact in a parallel universe. For example, if you prevent the assassination of Archduke Franz Ferdinand, it may not necessarily prevent the outbreak of World War I in a parallel universe.

Another challenge is the potential for paradoxes. In our universe, causality ensures that events occur in a specific order. However, in a multiverse where every possible outcome exists, it is possible to create paradoxes where an event causes itself. For example, if you traveled back in time and prevented your parents from meeting, you would never have been born. However, if you were never born, you could never have traveled back in time to prevent your parents from meeting. This creates a paradox that cannot be resolved.

Despite these challenges, the concept of the multiverse has significant implications for our understanding of time travel. It suggests that altering the past may not have the catastrophic consequences we once thought it would. Instead, it opens up the possibility of exploring new timelines and potentially improving the course of history.

As we continue to explore the possibilities of time travel, the concept of the multiverse will likely play an increasingly important role in shaping our understanding of the potential risks and benefits of altering the course of history. While the idea of time travel may still be firmly rooted in science fiction, the underlying physics behind it continues to intrigue scientists and inspire new research. Who knows what the future holds.

One area of research that may help us better understand the multiverse and the implications of time travel is quantum mechanics. The principles of quantum mechanics suggest that particles can exist in multiple states simultaneously, and that the act of observing a particle can cause it to collapse into a specific state. This has led some scientists to suggest that the act of traveling back in time and altering the past could be viewed as a quantum measurement, causing a collapse of the wave function and the creation of a new universe.

Another area of research that may shed light on the multiverse and time travel is the study of black holes. Black holes are some of the most mysterious and powerful objects in the universe, and scientists believe that they may hold the key to understanding the nature of time and space. One theory suggests that black holes could be portals to other universes, allowing us to travel through the multiverse and potentially even through time.

While these theories remain speculative, they highlight the ongoing fascination with the concept of time travel and the multiverse. They also underscore the importance of exploring these concepts in order to better understand the nature of the universe and our place within it.

Beyond the realm of science, the concept of the multiverse and time travel has captured the imagination of artists and writers. From science fiction novels to blockbuster films, the idea of exploring new timelines and parallel universes has inspired countless works of art.

One particularly popular depiction of time travel and the multiverse is the Back to the Future film franchise. The films explore the concept of altering the past and the potential consequences of doing so, while also incorporating humor and adventure. They have become cultural touchstones and continue to inspire new generations of fans.

Another popular work of science fiction that explores the multiverse and time travel is the book and TV series, "The Man in the High Castle" by Philip K. Dick. The story imagines a world where the Axis powers won World War II and the United States is divided between Japan and Germany. The protagonist discovers a film reel that shows an alternate reality where the Allies won the war, leading him on a journey to discover the true nature of reality.

These works of art and entertainment highlight the enduring appeal of the concept of time travel and the multiverse. They allow us to explore new worlds and possibilities, while also reminding us of the importance of the choices we make and the impact they can have.

The concept of the multiverse is one of the most intriguing and complex ideas in modern physics. It suggests the existence of an infinite number of parallel universes, each containing a different outcome of every event. This has significant implications for the potential of time travel, suggesting that altering the past could create a new parallel universe rather than affecting our own.

While the concept of the multiverse remains purely theoretical at this point, it continues to fascinate scientists and inspire new research. It also captures the imagination of artists and writers, who use it as a jumping-off point for exploring new worlds and possibilities.

As we continue to explore the concept of time travel and the multiverse, we will undoubtedly encounter new challenges and questions. However, the ongoing pursuit of understanding the nature of the universe and our place within it is a worthy endeavor that will continue to captivate us for generations to come.

One area of research that may further our understanding of the multiverse and time travel is the study of dark energy. Dark energy is a mysterious force that is believed to be responsible for the accelerating expansion of the universe. Some scientists have proposed that the existence of dark energy could be evidence of the multiverse, as it could be the result of energy leaking between parallel universes.

The study of dark energy has the potential to unlock new insights into the nature of the multiverse and our ability to travel through it. It could also lead to new discoveries in our understanding of the fundamental forces of the universe and the nature of reality itself.

Another area of research that is closely related to the concept of the multiverse and time travel is the study of wormholes. Wormholes are theoretical passages through space-time that could potentially allow us to travel vast distances or even traverse the multiverse.

The study of wormholes is still in its early stages, and there are many unanswered questions and technical challenges that must be overcome. However, the potential benefits of understanding wormholes and their relationship to the multiverse and time travel are immense.

As we continue to explore the possibilities of the multiverse and time travel, it is important to consider the ethical implications of altering the course of history. While the creation of a new parallel universe may seem like a relatively benign outcome, it is still possible that our actions in that universe could have unintended consequences.

In addition, the ability to travel through time and alter the past could be a powerful tool in the wrong hands. It is important to consider the potential risks and benefits of time travel and the multiverse carefully, and to use this knowledge responsibly.

Ultimately, the concept of the multiverse and time travel reminds us of the infinite possibilities that exist within the universe. It challenges us to explore new frontiers and to question our assumptions about the nature of reality.

Whether we ever discover a way to travel through time and traverse the multiverse remains to be seen. However, the ongoing pursuit of these ideas will undoubtedly lead to new discoveries and a deeper understanding of the universe we call home.

In the end, it is up to us to decide how we will use this knowledge and what kind of future we will create for ourselves and future generations. The possibilities are endless, and the future is ours to shape.

While the concept of time travel and the multiverse may seem like science fiction, there are already some practical applications that we can explore. One such application is the concept of virtual reality.

Virtual reality technology allows us to create immersive digital environments that we can explore and interact with. While virtual reality may seem like a far cry from the concept of time travel and the multiverse, it allows us to experience simulated environments and scenarios that would otherwise be impossible.

For example, virtual reality technology could be used to simulate historical events or even hypothetical scenarios that explore the potential consequences of altering the course of history. This could help us better understand the potential risks and benefits of time travel and the multiverse and make more informed decisions about our actions.

Another potential application of virtual reality technology is in the field of space exploration. Virtual reality simulations could allow us to explore the vast expanse of space and even simulate the experience of traveling through a wormhole or traversing the multiverse.

Of course, virtual reality is still in its early stages, and there are many technical and ethical challenges that must be overcome before it can reach its full potential. However, the potential applications of this technology in the field of time travel and the multiverse are exciting and could have a significant impact on our understanding of the universe.

As we continue to advance our knowledge and understanding of the fundamental forces of the universe, we may one day unlock the secrets of time travel and the multiverse. This knowledge could have a profound impact on our understanding of reality and our ability to shape the future.

In the end, it is up to us to decide how we will use this knowledge and what kind of future we will create for ourselves and future generations. The possibilities are endless, and the future is ours to shape. The journey towards unlocking the secrets of the multiverse and time travel is just beginning, and the potential rewards are immense.

The concept of time travel has been a fascinating subject for scientists and science fiction writers alike for decades. It has captured our imaginations, and we have been trying to unlock its secrets for as long as we have known about it. But what if time travel could have significant implications beyond just going back in time to change history? What if the very fabric of reality itself could be altered by time travel? This is where the concept of the multiverse comes in.

The multiverse theory is one of the most intriguing concepts in modern physics. It suggests the existence of an infinite number of parallel universes, each one containing every possible outcome of every event. This means that if time travel were possible, any changes made to the past would not affect our own universe but would instead create a new parallel universe. This theory has significant implications for the potential risks and consequences of time travel.

Imagine you could go back in time and change something significant, like preventing the assassination of a prominent historical figure. In our current universe, the consequences of such an action could be disastrous. The outcome could be vastly different from what we know to be true, potentially causing catastrophic changes to the course of history. However, in a parallel universe, the outcome could be entirely different. It is possible that the changes made could have less severe or even positive outcomes. The multiverse theory suggests that every possible outcome exists in its own universe, which means that the potential for positive change is also possible.

Of course, the multiverse theory remains purely hypothetical at this point, and there is no way to confirm its existence or the potential implications for time travel. However, the idea that we could be altering the very fabric of reality itself is a tantalizing prospect that continues to fascinate scientists and science fiction writers alike.

Despite the lack of concrete evidence for the multiverse theory, some scientists believe that it could be the key to unlocking the secrets of time travel. They suggest that the existence of parallel universes could provide a way to avoid the paradoxes and inconsistencies that would arise from changing the past in our own universe. By creating a new parallel universe with each change, the original universe remains intact, and the consequences of time travel are limited to the new universe.

But how do we know that these parallel universes exist? The idea of the multiverse comes from several different theories, including string theory and the many-worlds interpretation of quantum mechanics. While these theories have yet to be proven definitively, they have gained significant traction in the scientific community.

String theory suggests that the universe is made up of multiple dimensions, each one representing a different possible outcome of an event. The many-worlds interpretation of quantum mechanics, on the other hand, suggests that every time a quantum measurement is made, the universe splits into multiple parallel universes, each one representing a different outcome.

While the idea of multiple dimensions and parallel universes may seem far-fetched, there is some evidence to support it. For example, the famous double-slit experiment, which demonstrated the wave-particle duality of light, suggests that particles exist in a superposition of states until observed, at which point they collapse into a single state. This has led some scientists to suggest that the act of observation could be creating parallel universes.

While the multiverse theory remains a fascinating concept with many potential implications, it is important to remember that it is still purely hypothetical at this point. There is no concrete evidence to support its existence, and it is possible that it may never be proven definitively. However, even if the multiverse theory turns out to be nothing more than a fascinating idea, it has already had a significant impact on our understanding of time travel and the potential risks and benefits of altering the course of history.

For example, if we were to go back in time and prevent a significant historical event, would we be erasing an important part of our collective history? Would we be denying future generations the opportunity to learn from the mistakes of the past? On the other hand, if we were to go back in time and prevent a catastrophic event, such as a global disaster, would we not have a moral obligation to do so?

The multiverse theory also raises questions about free will and determinism. If every possible outcome exists in its own universe, does that mean that our lives are predetermined? If so, what does that mean for the concept of free will? These are complex philosophical questions that have yet to be fully explored.

Despite these questions and concerns, the concept of the multiverse remains an intriguing possibility that continues to fascinate scientists and science fiction writers alike. It has inspired countless books, movies, and TV shows, each one exploring the possibilities and implications of parallel universes.

One of the most famous examples of this is the Back to the Future trilogy, which explores the consequences of altering the past and the potential for creating new parallel universes. The popular TV show, Fringe, also explores the concept of parallel universes, with the characters traveling between different versions of reality in an attempt to save their own.

The concept of the multiverse has also had a significant impact on our understanding of the universe as a whole. It has led scientists to explore the possibility of multiple universes existing alongside our own, each one with its own unique physical laws and constants. This has opened up new avenues of research in the field of cosmology, with scientists attempting to discover evidence for the existence of these other universes.

In conclusion, the concept of the multiverse remains one of the most intriguing and fascinating ideas in modern physics. While it remains purely hypothetical at this point, it has significant implications for the potential of time travel and our understanding of the universe as a whole. It raises important questions about ethics, free will, and determinism, and has inspired countless works of science fiction. As we continue to explore the possibilities of time travel and the multiverse, we are sure to uncover new and exciting discoveries that will change our understanding of the universe forever.

The concept of the multiverse has also inspired new avenues of research in the field of quantum mechanics. Some scientists believe that the multiverse theory could help explain the strange behavior of subatomic particles, such as quantum entanglement and superposition. They propose that the particles exist in multiple universes simultaneously, and that their behavior is influenced by interactions with particles in other universes.

While this remains a controversial theory, it highlights the potential for the multiverse concept to revolutionize our understanding of the fundamental workings of the universe. It also underscores the interconnectedness of all things, even across different universes.

In addition to its scientific implications, the multiverse theory has also had a significant impact on popular culture. It has inspired countless works of fiction, from movies and TV shows to books and video games. Some of the most famous examples include the Marvel Cinematic Universe, which features alternate realities and timelines, and the DC Comics multiverse, which includes different versions of popular characters from various parallel universes.

The multiverse has also had an impact on the way we think about reality itself. It raises important philosophical questions about the nature of existence and the meaning of life. If there are infinite versions of reality, does that mean that anything and everything is possible? And if so, what does that mean for our own existence?

The multiverse theory also has implications for our understanding of consciousness and the nature of the self. If there are infinite versions of ourselves in different parallel universes, does that mean that we are all connected in some way? And if so, what does that mean for our own sense of identity and individuality?

As we continue to explore the possibilities of the multiverse theory, we are sure to uncover new and exciting discoveries that will change the way we think about the universe and our place within it. Whether we are exploring the potential for time travel or delving into the mysteries of quantum mechanics, the multiverse theory remains one of the most fascinating and thought-provoking concepts in modern physics.

The multiverse theory is a theoretical construct that suggests the existence of an infinite number of parallel universes. This concept has significant implications for the potential of time travel and has raised important questions about ethics, free will, and determinism. It has inspired new avenues of research in the fields of cosmology and quantum mechanics, and has had a significant impact on popular culture and our understanding of reality itself. As we continue to explore the possibilities of the multiverse, we are sure to uncover new and exciting discoveries that will change our understanding of the universe forever.

# 8. Ripples in the Fabric of Time Travel

The concept of the butterfly effect, first proposed by mathematician and meteorologist Edward Lorenz in the 1960s, suggests that small changes in initial conditions can have significant and unpredictable effects on complex systems.

This concept has significant implications for the potential risks and consequences of time travel. Even small changes made in the past could have significant and unpredictable effects on the course of history and the present day.

For example, preventing a single event or changing a small detail in the past could potentially lead to a vastly different present day, with unintended consequences and unforeseen ripple effects.

This raises important ethical concerns about the potential impact of time travel on the natural order of time and space. Any changes made to the past must be carefully considered and weighed against the potential risks and consequences.

Despite these challenges, the concept of the butterfly effect also highlights the potential benefits of time travel. By making small changes in the past, we may be able to alter the course of history in positive ways and prevent disasters and tragedies before they occur.

As we continue to explore the possibilities of time travel, it is important that we do so with a careful and thoughtful approach that takes into account the potential risks and benefits of altering the natural order of time and space.

The butterfly effect is a fascinating concept that has been around for decades. It was first introduced by mathematician and meteorologist Edward Lorenz in the 1960s, and it suggests that small changes in initial conditions can have significant and unpredictable effects on complex systems. This means that even the smallest changes can lead to major consequences, and it has significant implications for time travel.

The butterfly effect has been popularized in popular culture and has become a staple of science fiction. The idea that changing a small detail in the past can lead to significant changes in the present has captured the imagination of writers and readers alike. However, the concept also raises important ethical concerns about the potential impact of time travel on the natural order of time and space.

Preventing a single event or changing a small detail in the past could potentially lead to a vastly different present day, with unintended consequences and unforeseen ripple effects. For example, preventing a natural disaster may seem like a noble goal, but it could also have unintended consequences. Perhaps the disaster was necessary to prevent an even greater catastrophe, or perhaps it played a vital role in shaping the course of history.

For example, if we were able to go back in time and prevent the assassination of Archduke Franz Ferdinand, could we have prevented World War I and the deaths of millions of people? Or, if we were able to go back in time and warn the people of Pompeii of the impending eruption of Mount Vesuvius, could we have saved thousands of lives?

One of the challenges of time travel is that it is inherently paradoxical. The idea of going back in time and changing the past raises questions about causality and the nature of time itself. If we change the past, does that mean that the present is no longer the present? Does it mean that our actions in the present have no consequences?

The paradoxical nature of time travel has been explored in popular culture, with movies like "Back to the Future" and

"The Terminator" presenting their own interpretations of how time travel works. However, the true nature of time travel remains a subject of speculation and debate.

Another challenge of time travel is the question of how it would affect free will. If we go back in time and change the course of history, are we taking away the free will of the people who were originally involved in those events? If we prevent a tragedy, are we taking away the agency of those who were meant to suffer through it?

The question of free will is a complex one, and it is closely tied to the idea of determinism. If we believe that the future is determined by the past, then changing the past could have significant implications for the future. However, if we believe in free will and the ability of individuals to make choices, then time travel could be seen as a way to give people a second chance to make different choices.

The potential benefits and risks of time travel are complex and multifaceted, and they require careful consideration

One of the ways in which we can approach the potential risks and benefits of time travel is by exploring the different types of time travel. There are several different types of time travel that are commonly depicted in science fiction, each with their own unique challenges and implications.

The first type of time travel is the "fixed timeline" model, in which time is seen as fixed and unchangeable. This model suggests that any attempts to change the past will ultimately fail, as the events that have already occurred are already set in stone. This type of time travel is often depicted in movies like "Harry Potter and the Prisoner of Azkaban," where time travel is used to ensure that the past events occur as they were meant to.

The second type of time travel is the "multiverse" model, in which time travel creates multiple parallel universes or timelines. This model suggests that any changes made to the past will result in a new timeline branching off from the original timeline. This type of time travel is often depicted in movies like "Star Trek" and "Doctor Who," where characters travel through time and encounter alternate versions of themselves and alternate timelines.

The third type of time travel is the "ripple effect" model, in which small changes in the past can have significant and unpredictable effects on the present. This model is closely tied to the concept of the butterfly effect, and it suggests that even small changes made to the past can have significant and far-reaching consequences. This type of time travel is often depicted in movies like "The Butterfly Effect" and "Groundhog Day."

Each of these types of time travel presents its own unique challenges and implications, and it is important to consider the potential risks and benefits of each type when exploring the possibility of time travel.

Another challenge of time travel is the potential for unintended consequences. Even if we are able to make changes in the past that have positive effects on the present, there is always the risk that those changes could have unintended consequences further down the line. For example, preventing a natural disaster may seem like a noble goal, but it could also have unintended consequences. Perhaps the disaster was necessary to prevent an even greater catastrophe, or perhaps it played a vital role in shaping the course of history.

The potential for unintended consequences highlights the importance of approaching time travel with caution and a thorough understanding of the potential risks and benefits. Any changes made to the past must be carefully considered and weighed against the potential risks, and the potential for unintended consequences must be taken into account.

Despite the challenges and potential risks of time travel, the concept remains a fascinating subject of exploration and speculation. As we continue to explore the possibilities of time travel, it is important that we do so with a careful and thoughtful approach that takes into account the potential risks and benefits of altering the natural order of time and space.

One of the ways in which we can approach the potential risks and benefits of time travel is by exploring the different ethical frameworks that can be applied to the concept. There are several different ethical frameworks that can be used to evaluate the potential risks and benefits of time travel, each with its own unique perspective on the issue.

One ethical framework that can be applied to time travel is utilitarianism, which suggests that the right course of action is the one that results in the greatest overall benefit to society. Using this framework, we could evaluate the potential risks and benefits of time travel based on their impact on society as a whole.

Another ethical framework that can be applied to time travel is deontology, which suggests that the right course of action is the one that is based on a set of moral principles or rules. Using this framework, we could evaluate the potential risks and benefits of time travel based on their alignment with a set of moral principles.

A third ethical framework that can be applied to time travel is virtue ethics, which suggests that the right course of action is the one that reflects the virtues and character of the individual or society involved. Using this framework, we could evaluate the potential risks and benefits of time travel based on how they reflect our values and virtues.

Each of these ethical frameworks provides a unique perspective on the potential risks and benefits of time travel, and it is important to consider each of them when evaluating the issue.

One of the potential benefits of time travel is the ability to prevent disasters and tragedies before they occur. By traveling back in time and making small changes, we may be able to prevent events like natural disasters, wars, and terrorist attacks, potentially saving countless lives.

However, as previously mentioned, there is always the potential for unintended consequences. Preventing a disaster may seem like a noble goal, but it could also have unintended consequences further down the line. For example, preventing a war may seem like a positive outcome, but it could also have unintended consequences such as leading to a rise of a different form of conflict or instability.

Another potential benefit of time travel is the ability to gain knowledge and insights from the past. By traveling back in time and observing historical events firsthand, we may be able to gain a deeper understanding of our own history and culture, and potentially learn important lessons that can be applied to the present day.

However, there is also the potential for misuse of this knowledge. For example, individuals or groups could use knowledge gained from the past to gain an unfair advantage in the present, or to manipulate events for their own gain.

The potential risks and benefits of time travel are complex and multifaceted, and it is important to consider them from multiple perspectives. This includes considering the scientific, philosophical, and ethical implications of time travel, as well as the potential impact on society as a whole.

Despite the challenges and potential risks, the concept of time travel remains a fascinating subject of exploration and speculation. Whether it is through science fiction or real-world scientific research, the exploration of time travel offers a glimpse into the potential of humanity's imagination and innovation.

The implications of the butterfly effect on time travel are profound. It means that any changes made to the past must be carefully considered and weighed against the potential risks and consequences. It also means that time travel is not a simple matter of going back in time and making changes. Instead, it requires a careful and thoughtful approach that takes into account the potential risks and benefits of altering the natural order of time and space.

However, even positive changes made in the past could have unintended consequences. For example, preventing a war could lead to a different set of problems that we cannot predict. This is why time travel requires a careful and thoughtful approach that takes into account the potential risks and benefits of altering the natural order of time and space.

One potential way to minimize the risks of time travel is to limit the changes made to the past. Instead of making major changes that could alter the course of history, we could make small changes that have a limited impact. For example, we could prevent a single person from making a mistake that caused a disaster, or we could provide assistance to people in the past who were suffering.

Another way to minimize the risks of time travel is to carefully monitor the changes made to the past. This would require a sophisticated system that tracks the changes made and the potential consequences of those changes. It would also require a team of experts who can analyze the data and make decisions about whether to continue with the changes or revert to the original timeline.

In addition to the ethical concerns raised by the butterfly effect, there are also practical concerns. Time travel may be physically impossible, or it may require technology that is currently beyond our understanding. Even if time travel is possible, it may be prohibitively expensive or dangerous. These practical concerns must also be taken into account when considering the potential risks and benefits of time travel.

Despite these challenges, the concept of the butterfly effect and its implications for time travel are fascinating and thought-provoking. As we continue to explore the possibilities of time travel, it is important that we do so with a careful and thoughtful approach that takes into account the potential risks and benefits of altering the natural order of time and space. By doing so, we may be able to unlock the secrets of the past and shape the course of the future in positive ways.

One potential use of time travel is to study history and gain a better understanding of past events. By observing the past firsthand, we may be able to gain new insights into historical events and better understand the motivations and actions of historical figures. This could help us avoid making the same mistakes in the future and make more informed decisions in the present day.

However, using time travel for historical research raises its own set of ethical concerns. For example, if we were to observe a historical event without being detected, we may be able to gain a better understanding of the event, but we would also be invading the privacy of the people who lived through it. It is important to carefully consider the potential benefits and risks of time travel for historical research.

Another potential use of time travel is to explore the future and gain insights into potential outcomes of present-day decisions. By traveling to the future, we may be able to see the consequences of our actions and make better decisions in the present day. However, this also raises ethical concerns about altering the future by observing it.

Ultimately, the concept of the butterfly effect and its implications for time travel highlight the interconnectedness of all things in the universe. Small changes in one part of the system can have significant and unpredictable effects on other parts of the system. This means that we must approach time travel with humility and caution, recognizing that our actions have consequences that we cannot always predict or control.

Furthermore, the concept of the butterfly effect also raises questions about free will and determinism. If small changes in initial conditions can have significant effects on the course of history and the present day, does that mean that our actions and choices are predetermined by the initial conditions of the universe? Or do we have free will to make choices that can alter the course of history and the future?

These are complex philosophical questions that have been debated for centuries, and the implications of time travel only add another layer to the discussion. Some argue that time travel is incompatible with free will, since any changes made to the past would ultimately be predetermined by the initial conditions of the universe. Others argue that time travel is compatible with free will, since it would allow us to make choices that can alter the course of history and the future.

Regardless of where one falls on this philosophical debate, it is clear that time travel is a fascinating concept that has captured the imaginations of people for generations. It has been explored in countless works of fiction, from H.G. Wells' "The Time Machine" to Christopher Nolan's "Tenet". However, the reality of time travel remains purely theoretical at this point, and there are many scientific and technological challenges that must be overcome before it becomes a reality.

One of the biggest challenges of time travel is the issue of causality. If we were able to travel back in time and make changes to the past, would those changes create paradoxes or inconsistencies in the timeline? For example, what would happen if we traveled back in time and prevented our own birth? Would we cease to exist, or would the timeline shift to accommodate our absence?

These are complex questions that have yet to be fully answered by science, and they highlight the need for a careful and thoughtful approach to time travel. It is important to consider the potential risks and consequences of altering the natural order of time and space, and to ensure that any advances in time travel technology are accompanied by rigorous ethical guidelines and regulations.

The concept of the butterfly effect and its implications for time travel are fascinating and thought-provoking. While time travel remains purely theoretical at this point, it is clear that it raises important ethical concerns and philosophical questions about the nature of time, space, and free will. As we continue to explore the possibilities of time travel, it is important that we do so with a careful and thoughtful approach that takes into account the potential risks and benefits of altering the natural order of the universe.

# 9. The Philosophy of Time Travel

The concept of time travel raises significant philosophical questions about the nature of time and our place in the universe. For example, the idea of traveling through time challenges our understanding of causality and free will.

One of the fundamental questions in the philosophy of time travel is whether the future is predetermined or whether we have the ability to change it. If time is linear and unchangeable, then time travel may be impossible, or at least limited to observation rather than interaction.

However, if time is malleable and subject to change, then the possibilities for time travel are much broader. This raises questions about the nature of causality and whether our actions in the past could have unintended consequences in the future.

The concept of free will also plays a significant role in the philosophy of time travel. If the future is predetermined, then it may be argued that we have no true agency in our actions and that all of our choices and decisions are predetermined. However, if we have the ability to alter the course of history, then we may have greater agency in shaping our own destiny.

These questions are not easily answered, and the philosophy of time travel remains a subject of intense debate and speculation. However, by grappling with these fundamental questions, we may gain a deeper understanding of the nature of time and our place in the universe.

The concept of time travel has long captured the human imagination. From science fiction novels to blockbuster movies, the idea of traveling through time has captivated audiences around the world. But beyond its entertainment value, time travel raises significant philosophical questions about the nature of time and our place in the universe.

At the heart of the philosophy of time travel is the question of whether time is linear or malleable. If time is linear and unchangeable, then time travel may be limited to observation rather than interaction. However, if time is malleable and subject to change, then the possibilities for time travel are much broader.

This raises questions about the nature of causality and whether our actions in the past could have unintended consequences in the future. If the future is predetermined, then it may be argued that we have no true agency in our actions and that all of our choices and decisions are predetermined.

The concept of free will also plays a significant role in the philosophy of time travel. If the future is predetermined, then it may be argued that we have no true agency in our actions and that all of our choices and decisions are predetermined. However, if we have the ability to alter the course of history, then we may have greater agency in shaping our own destiny.

On the other hand, if time is malleable and subject to change, then the possibilities for time travel are much broader. This raises questions about the nature of causality and whether our actions in the past could have unintended consequences in the future.

If time is malleable, then it may be possible to change the course of history and alter the future. However, this raises further questions about the ethics of time travel and the potential consequences of altering the past.

The potential consequences of altering the past raise significant ethical questions about the use of time travel. If time travel were possible, who would have access to it and who would be responsible for its use?

The ethical implications of time travel are far-reaching and complex. For example, if a time traveler were to go back in time and change the course of history, would they be morally responsible for the consequences of that change? Should time travel be regulated and controlled to prevent potentially harmful changes to the past?

The concept of time travel raises significant philosophical questions about the nature of time and our place in the universe. Whether time is linear or malleable, the possibilities for time travel are both fascinating and complex.

The philosophy of time travel raises questions about causality, free will, and the ethics of altering the past. While the concept of time travel may seem like science fiction, its philosophical implications have real-world relevance and are worthy of serious consideration.

As we continue to explore the nature of time and our place in the universe, the philosophy of time travel will undoubtedly remain a subject of fascination and debate.

The nature of time travel also raises questions about the nature of reality itself. If time is malleable, then what is the nature of the past, present, and future? Are they all equally real, or is there a fundamental difference between them?

One popular view of time is that it is like a river, with past events flowing downstream and future events flowing upstream. This view suggests that the past is fixed and unchangeable, while the future is open and subject to change.

However, the concept of time travel challenges this view of time. If time travel were possible, it would suggest that the past is not fixed and unchangeable, but rather malleable and subject to alteration. This raises questions about the nature of time and the nature of reality itself.

Another philosophical question raised by time travel is the concept of personal identity. If we were to travel back in time and meet our younger selves, would we still be the same person? Or would we be a different person altogether?

The concept of time travel also raises questions about the limits of scientific knowledge. While time travel is often depicted in popular culture as a purely scientific pursuit, it is unclear whether it is even possible according to our current understanding of physics. The question of whether time travel is possible is an ongoing subject of scientific inquiry and debate.

One possible way that time travel could be achieved is through the use of wormholes. Wormholes are theoretical tunnels in space-time that could potentially allow us to travel vast distances in a short amount of time. However, the technology required to create and navigate wormholes is currently beyond our reach.

The philosophy of time travel also has implications for the search for extraterrestrial life. If time travel were possible, it could potentially allow us to travel back in time and observe historical events on other planets. This could provide valuable insights into the history of life in the universe.

Overall, the philosophy of time travel raises many fascinating questions about the nature of time, the nature of reality, and the limits of scientific knowledge. While time travel may seem like science fiction, its philosophical implications have real-world relevance and are worthy of serious consideration.

As we continue to explore the nature of time and our place in the universe, the philosophy of time travel will undoubtedly remain a subject of fascination and debate. Whether time travel is possible or not, it offers us a unique window into the mysteries of the universe and the nature of our existence.

One important aspect of the philosophy of time travel is the idea of paradoxes. Paradoxes occur when time travelers make changes in the past that end up affecting their own present or future. For example, the grandfather paradox states that if a time traveler were to go back in time and kill their own grandfather before they had children, they would never be born, and therefore could not have traveled back in time to kill their grandfather.

The existence of such paradoxes raises questions about the nature of causality and the possibility of altering the past. If time travel were possible, would the very act of traveling back in time be enough to alter the course of history, or would the timeline remain unchanged?

The concept of time travel also has implications for our understanding of the nature of reality. If time is malleable and subject to change, then what is the true nature of reality? Is it fixed and unchanging, or is it constantly shifting and evolving based on our actions and decisions?

One theory of time travel suggests that it may be possible to travel to alternate timelines or parallel universes, where events unfold differently than in our own timeline. This would suggest that there are multiple versions of reality, each with its own unique timeline and set of events.

The philosophy of time travel also raises ethical questions about the responsibility of time travelers. If time travel were possible, what responsibilities would time travelers have to the people and events of the past? Would they have a duty to preserve history as it happened, or would they have the right to alter it for their own purposes?

One possible scenario is that time travel could be used to prevent tragedies and disasters from occurring. For example, a time traveler could go back in time to prevent a natural disaster or terrorist attack. However, this raises questions about the potential unintended consequences of such actions and whether the time traveler would have the right to alter the course of history in such a significant way.

Another ethical consideration is the potential impact of time travel on future generations. If time travel were possible, it could potentially create a feedback loop in which the actions of time travelers in the past affect the future, which then leads to further time travel and alterations to the timeline. This could create a situation where future generations are constantly dealing with the unintended consequences of past time travel.

The philosophy of time travel raises many fascinating questions about the nature of time, the nature of reality, and the limits of human knowledge and understanding. While time travel may seem like a purely hypothetical concept, its philosophical implications have real-world relevance and are worthy of serious consideration.

As we continue to explore the mysteries of the universe and our place in it, the philosophy of time travel will undoubtedly remain a subject of fascination and debate. While the possibility of time travel may be uncertain, its philosophical implications offer us a unique window into the nature of our existence and the mysteries of the universe.

Advancements in science and technology may one day allow us to explore the concept of time travel in more depth. While time travel remains firmly in the realm of science fiction for now, scientists are beginning to explore the idea of manipulating time on a smaller scale.

For example, researchers have conducted experiments with time dilation, in which the passage of time is slowed down or sped up using high-speed travel or gravitational fields. These experiments have demonstrated that time is not a fixed and constant quantity, but is instead subject to the effects of motion and gravity.

Similarly, quantum mechanics offers the possibility of time travel on a small scale, through the phenomenon of quantum entanglement. This occurs when two particles become linked in such a way that the state of one particle affects the state of the other, regardless of the distance between them. Some scientists have suggested that this phenomenon could be used to send information back in time, although this remains purely theoretical for now.

As our understanding of the nature of time and the universe continues to evolve, it is possible that we may one day find ways to explore the concept of time travel more fully. However, this also raises questions about the potential dangers and risks of time travel, and whether the benefits would outweigh the potential consequences.

For example, if time travel were possible, it could potentially be used for nefarious purposes, such as altering historical events for personal gain or power. This could lead to a rewriting of history and a distortion of our understanding of the past.

Furthermore, time travel could potentially create paradoxes and contradictions that would be difficult to reconcile. For example, if a time traveler were to go back in time and change a key event, such as preventing a major disaster, this could potentially create a paradox in which the disaster never occurred, and therefore the time traveler would never have been motivated to go back in time to prevent it in the first place.

Despite these potential dangers, the concept of time travel remains a subject of fascination and intrigue for scientists and philosophers alike. It challenges our understanding of the universe and our place within it, and offers a unique perspective on the nature of time, causality, and free will.

In the end, the question of whether time travel is possible may never be fully resolved. But regardless of its feasibility, the philosophy of time travel will continue to inspire new ideas, theories, and debates, and will remain a fascinating subject for generations to come.

Time travel has captured the imagination of humans for centuries. From H.G. Wells' "The Time Machine" to "Doctor Who," we've seen many versions of time travel in literature and media. But the idea of traveling through time raises significant philosophical questions about the nature of time itself and our place in the universe.

At the heart of the philosophy of time travel is the question of whether the future is predetermined or whether we have the ability to change it. If time is linear and unchangeable, then time travel may be impossible, or at least limited to observation rather than interaction. In other words, we could observe the past or future, but we would be unable to change anything.

The concept of causality is also central to the philosophy of time travel. Causality refers to the relationship between an event (the cause) and a second event (the effect), where the second event is understood as a consequence of the first. If time is linear and unchangeable, then the concept of causality is straightforward: every effect has a cause, and every cause has a specific effect. However, if time is malleable and subject to change, then the concept of causality becomes more complex. In a world where the future can be changed, our actions in the past could have unintended consequences in the future, making it difficult to predict the outcome of our choices.

Free will is also an important consideration when it comes to the philosophy of time travel. If the future is predetermined, then it may be argued that we have no true agency in our actions and that all of our choices and decisions are predetermined. However, if we have the ability to alter the course of history, then we may have greater agency in shaping our own destiny.

The philosopher David Lewis proposed a theory of time travel that takes into account the concept of causality. Lewis suggested that if time travel were possible, then we could travel back in time and change the past, but only in a way that is consistent with the causal structure of the universe. In other words, we could make changes, but we could not create paradoxes or inconsistencies in the timeline.

This raises the question of whether time travel is even possible. While time travel is a popular theme in science fiction, there is currently no scientific evidence to suggest that it is possible. The laws of physics, as we understand them, do not allow for time travel, and the concept of causality would make time travel incredibly difficult to achieve. However, as our understanding of the universe continues to evolve, it is possible that we may discover new technologies or new understandings of physics that make time travel a reality.

Regardless of whether time travel is possible or not, the philosophy of time travel remains a fascinating subject of study. By grappling with fundamental questions about the nature of time and our place in the universe, we gain a deeper understanding of the world around us.

One of the most significant implications of time travel is the possibility of changing the course of history. If time travel were possible, then we could potentially prevent catastrophic events from occurring, such as the assassination of a political leader or the outbreak of a deadly disease. However, this raises ethical questions about the potential consequences of altering the timeline. Would changing the past create unintended consequences in the future? Would it create new problems or exacerbate existing ones? These questions are difficult to answer, but they are important to consider when thinking about the implications of time travel.

Another interesting aspect of time travel is the concept of multiple timelines. In many works of science fiction, time travel is portrayed as creating alternate timelines or universes, where the choices made by time travelers result in a new reality that is distinct from the original timeline. This raises questions about the nature of reality itself and whether there is a single, objective reality or whether reality is subjective and contingent on the choices we make. If there are multiple timelines or universes, then it may be possible to explore different versions of reality and learn more about the potential outcomes of different choices and actions.

The idea of multiple timelines also raises questions about identity and personal continuity. If we were to travel back in time and change something about our past, would we still be the same person? Would our memories and experiences still be valid, or would they be altered by the changes we've made to the timeline? These questions touch on the nature of personal identity and whether our identity is determined by our past experiences or by some other factor.

Another interesting philosophical question related to time travel is whether time itself is an objective reality or a subjective experience. Many philosophers have argued that time is a human construct and that it does not exist as an objective reality in the same way that space does. If time is subjective, then the concept of time travel becomes even more complex, as it may involve not just traveling through space but also through different perceptions of time.

The philosophy of time travel also has implications for our understanding of the universe as a whole. If time travel were possible, then it may be possible to explore different periods of the universe's history and gain new insights into its origins and evolution. This could have significant implications for our understanding of cosmology and the nature of the universe.

Time travel is a fascinating concept that has intrigued scientists, philosophers, and writers for centuries. It's the idea that we can travel through time, either backward or forward, and change events or see the future. While time travel remains a popular topic in science fiction, it's also an area of interest for physicists and philosophers. The concept of time travel raises many questions about the nature of time and reality, the concept of personal identity, and our understanding of the universe as a whole.

The concept of multiple timelines suggests that there are multiple versions of reality coexisting simultaneously. Each time an event occurs, it creates a new timeline. Therefore, if we were to travel back in time and change something, we would create a new timeline. In this new timeline, we may not even exist or have different experiences, memories, and personality traits.

The idea of multiple timelines also raises questions about the nature of causality. If we were to travel back in time and change something, would it have a ripple effect on the future? Would the changes we've made in the past create a new future, or would they simply create a new timeline that runs parallel to our own? These questions touch on the fundamental nature of cause and effect, and whether events are predetermined or can be changed.

Time travel has been a popular subject in science fiction literature and films for decades. However, the concept of time travel raises many philosophical questions that are not just confined to the realm of fiction. One of the most interesting philosophical questions related to time travel is whether time itself is an objective reality or a subjective experience. Many philosophers have argued that time is a human construct and that it does not exist as an objective reality in the same way that space does. According to this view, time is simply a mental construct.

The concept of time has been a subject of philosophical inquiry for centuries. The ancient Greeks, for example, believed in the idea of eternal time, which was seen as an unchanging and continuous flow. Aristotle, one of the most influential philosophers in history, believed that time was a measure of change and that it only existed in relation to change. He argued that time could not exist without change, and that change could not exist without time. This idea of time as a measure of change has been a central concept in philosophy ever since.

In the modern era, philosophers have continued to explore the nature of time and its relationship to the world around us. Some philosophers, like Immanuel Kant, have argued that time is a necessary condition for human experience. Kant believed that time was a priori, meaning that it was a fundamental aspect of human cognition and perception. He argued that time was not a property of the world itself, but rather a way that our minds organize and structure our experience of the world.

Other philosophers have taken a different approach to the concept of time. Some, like Gottfried Leibniz, have argued that time is an illusion and that it does not exist as an objective reality. Leibniz believed that time was simply a mental construct that we use to make sense of our experiences. He argued that time was not a property of the world, but rather a way that our minds organize and structure our experiences.

The debate over the nature of time has continued into the present day, with many contemporary philosophers offering their own perspectives on the subject. One of the most interesting questions related to time travel is whether time itself is an objective reality or a subjective experience. If time is an objective reality, then time travel is theoretically possible. If time is a subjective experience, then time travel may be nothing more than a mental construct.

Many philosophers who take the view that time is a human construct argue that time travel is impossible. According to this view, time is not a property of the world, but rather a way that our minds organize and structure our experiences. Therefore, the idea of traveling through time is simply a mental construct and not a real possibility.

However, there are other philosophers who believe that time is an objective reality and that time travel is theoretically possible. According to this view, time exists independently of human consciousness and is a fundamental aspect of the universe. Time travel, therefore, is not just a mental construct, but a real possibility.

One of the most influential theories related to the objective reality of time is the theory of relativity, proposed by Albert Einstein in the early 20th century. According to this theory, time is not absolute but rather relative to the observer. Time can be affected by gravity and the velocity of the observer. This means that time can appear to pass more slowly or more quickly depending on the observer's position in space and their velocity.

## 10.     The Evolving Landscape of Time Travel

As we look to the future, the possibilities for time travel are more exciting and intriguing than ever before. Advances in quantum computing, wormhole research, and other areas of physics may bring us closer than ever to unlocking the secrets of time.

However, with these exciting possibilities come significant challenges and risks. The potential impact on the natural order of time and space must be carefully considered, as well as the ethical implications of altering the course of history.

Despite these challenges, the potential benefits of time travel are significant. From exploring historical events firsthand to preventing disasters and tragedies before they occur, time travel could have a profound impact on the course of human history.

As we continue to explore the possibilities of time travel, it is important that we do so with a careful and thoughtful approach that takes into account the potential risks and benefits. By doing so, we may one day be able to unlock the unseen possibilities of time and reshape the course of history itself.

Time travel has been a topic of fascination for centuries, explored in literature, film, and television. From H.G. Wells' "The Time Machine" to the "Back to the Future" franchise, the idea of traveling through time has captured the imaginations of people around the world. However, time travel has long been considered a mere fantasy or a figment of science fiction. Yet, with recent advancements in physics, the possibility of time travel is becoming more real than ever before.

Advances in quantum computing, wormhole research, and other areas of physics have opened up new possibilities for time travel. In recent years, researchers have been able to manipulate individual atoms and control their quantum states, paving the way for new advancements in quantum computing. Scientists have also explored the concept of wormholes, which are hypothetical tunnels that connect two distant points in space and time. The idea is that if these tunnels can be created, then time travel might be possible.

The prospect of time travel is exciting and intriguing. Imagine being able to witness historical events firsthand or even prevent disasters and tragedies before they occur. Time travel could have a profound impact on the course of human history. However, with these exciting possibilities come significant challenges and risks.

The first and foremost challenge of time travel is the impact on the natural order of time and space. Time travel could create paradoxes that disrupt the laws of causality, such as the famous "grandfather paradox," in which someone travels back in time and accidentally prevents their grandfather from meeting their grandmother, thus rendering their own existence impossible. This kind of paradox would have profound consequences for the laws of nature and would require us to fundamentally rethink our understanding of the universe.

Another significant challenge of time travel is the ethical implications of altering the course of history. The butterfly effect, a concept popularized by the 2004 film of the same name, suggests that even the slightest change to the past could have catastrophic consequences for the present and future. Preventing tragedies, such as the assassination of JFK, might seem like a good thing, but it is impossible to predict the unintended consequences of altering history.

Moreover, the temptation to use time travel for personal gain or to rewrite history to suit one's own interests is a significant ethical concern. The very act of time travel would likely have significant psychological effects on the time traveler, potentially leading to feelings of disorientation, depression, or even insanity.

Despite these challenges, the potential benefits of time travel are significant. One of the most exciting possibilities of time travel is the ability to witness historical events firsthand. Imagine being able to watch the signing of the Declaration of Independence or see the construction of the Great Pyramids of Egypt. This kind of firsthand experience could provide new insights into our past and help us better understand the world we live in today.

Another potential benefit of time travel is the ability to prevent disasters before they occur. Imagine being able to go back in time and warn people about natural disasters such as hurricanes, earthquakes, or volcanic eruptions. Time travel could also be used to prevent man-made disasters such as terrorist attacks, wars, or pandemics.

Despite the potential benefits, the risks associated with time travel are significant. The disruption of the natural order of time and space, the ethical implications of altering history, and the psychological effects on the time traveler are all significant challenges that must be carefully considered.

Time travel has always been one of the most fascinating concepts in science fiction, literature, and entertainment. For centuries, people have been captivated by the idea of traveling through time and experiencing different eras firsthand. However, until recently, time travel was largely considered a fictional concept, a product of imagination and creative storytelling.

However, as science and technology have advanced, the possibility of time travel has become increasingly plausible. Scientists and physicists have made significant strides in understanding the nature of time and space, which has opened up new avenues for exploring the concept of time travel. With advances in quantum computing, wormhole research, and other areas of physics, the idea of traveling through time is no longer confined to the realm of science fiction but is slowly becoming a reality.

One of the key areas of research in time travel is quantum computing. Quantum computing is a type of computing that uses quantum-mechanical phenomena to perform calculations. Quantum computers are incredibly powerful and can perform certain calculations much faster than traditional computers. This makes them well-suited to tackle complex problems such as those related to time travel.

Another area of research is wormhole physics. A wormhole is a hypothetical shortcut through space and time that would allow someone to travel from one point in space to another point in space almost instantaneously. Wormholes have been a topic of scientific research for decades, and while they have yet to be proven to exist, they remain an intriguing area of study for physicists and scientists.

Despite these challenges, the potential benefits of time travel are significant. For one, time travel could provide us with a unique opportunity to explore historical events firsthand. Imagine being able to witness the signing of the Declaration of Independence or the landing on the moon. Time travel could also allow us to prevent disasters and tragedies before they occur, potentially saving countless lives and changing the course of human history for the better.

In recent years, researchers have explored the potential benefits of time travel in various fields. In medicine, time travel could help us better understand the evolution of diseases and develop more effective treatments. In finance, time travel could enable us to make better investment decisions by allowing us to see the outcome of different investment strategies over time. The possibilities are endless, and as we continue to explore the concept of time travel, new opportunities are likely to emerge.

However, as we delve further into the world of time travel, it is crucial that we do so with a careful and thoughtful approach. The potential risks and ethical implications must be considered carefully. Moreover, time travel research should be conducted with a long-term view, considering not just the immediate benefits but also the long-term impact on humanity.

Despite the challenges and risks of time travel, it remains a fascinating and intriguing concept. The idea of exploring different eras, preventing disasters, and changing the course of history is too tempting to ignore. As a result, many scientists and researchers are continuing to explore the possibilities of time travel, pushing the boundaries of science and technology to new heights.

One of the most exciting developments in time travel research is the possibility of time dilation. Time dilation occurs when an object is moving at a high speed or is in a strong gravitational field. As a result, time appears to slow down or speed up depending on the observer's position. This phenomenon has been observed in space travel, where astronauts on the International Space Station experience time dilation due to the station's high speed.

Another intriguing concept is the idea of multiple timelines. According to this theory, each decision we make creates a new timeline, leading to a multiverse of infinite possibilities. Time travel would allow us to explore these multiple timelines and potentially even travel between them. While this remains a highly theoretical concept, it has captured the imagination of many scientists and science fiction writers.

In recent years, time travel has become a popular subject in pop culture, with numerous movies, TV shows, and books exploring the concept. While many of these depictions are fictional and exaggerated, they have helped to popularize the idea of time travel and raise public awareness of ongoing time travel research.

However, as with any new technology, time travel brings with it potential dangers and risks. For example, time travel could be used as a tool for political gain, allowing individuals or governments to manipulate history for their own benefit. It could also be used to engage in criminal activity, such as stealing valuable artifacts from the past or committing crimes without fear of being caught.

Another potential risk is the impact on our mental health. Time travel could be a traumatic experience, exposing individuals to significant stress and anxiety. Moreover, it could create feelings of isolation and disorientation, as the time traveler struggles to adjust to a new environment and time period.

As we continue to explore the possibilities of time travel, it is crucial that we do so with a careful and thoughtful approach. We must consider the potential risks and benefits, as well as the ethical and moral implications of altering history. By doing so, we can ensure that time travel is used for the betterment of humanity, rather than for personal or political gain.

In conclusion, time travel remains one of the most fascinating and intriguing concepts in science and popular culture. Advances in science and technology have brought us closer than ever to unlocking the secrets of time travel, but significant challenges and risks remain. As we continue to explore the possibilities of time travel, it is important that we do so with a thoughtful and careful approach, considering not just the immediate benefits but also the long-term impact on humanity. By doing so, we may one day be able to unlock the unseen possibilities of time and reshape the course of human history itself.

Furthermore, the implications of time travel go beyond just the scientific and technological aspects. They also raise questions about our understanding of the nature of time itself and the philosophical implications of altering the course of history.

One of the key philosophical debates surrounding time travel is the concept of determinism versus free will. Determinism argues that everything that happens in the universe is predetermined and that the future is already set. Therefore, if time travel were possible, any attempt to change the course of history would ultimately be futile, as events would simply unfold as they were always meant to. On the other hand, free will argues that individuals have the power to make choices that can alter the course of history, and therefore time travel could potentially allow us to change the future.

Another important philosophical question is the idea of moral responsibility. If time travel were possible, would we have a responsibility to prevent tragedies and disasters from occurring? For example, if we could travel back in time to prevent the Holocaust or stop the September 11 attacks, would we have a moral obligation to do so? These are complex and difficult questions that require careful consideration and debate.

Moreover, the potential impact of time travel on our understanding of history and the way we interpret historical events is also significant. For example, if we were able to travel back in time and witness historical events firsthand, our understanding and interpretation of those events could change drastically. This could have profound implications for how we understand and teach history, as well as how we remember and memorialize historical figures and events.

The impact of time travel on our concept of personal identity is also an important consideration. If we were to travel back in time and meet our younger selves, would we be the same person, or would we be different individuals entirely? This raises questions about the continuity of personal identity and the way in which time shapes our understanding of ourselves.

Time travel is an exciting and intriguing possibility that could have a profound impact on the course of human history. Advances in quantum computing, wormhole research, and other areas of physics may bring us closer than ever to unlocking the secrets of time. However, the challenges and risks associated with time travel cannot be ignored. It is essential that we approach the possibility of time travel with a careful and thoughtful approach that takes into account the potential risks and benefits.

One way to approach the challenges of time travel is through the lens of ethics. Philosophers have long debated the morality of time travel, and many have argued that it is inherently wrong to interfere with the natural course of history. Others argue that if time travel is possible, it is our duty to use it for the betterment of humanity.

One ethical consideration is the potential for time travel to create a kind of "time imperialism." If time travel were possible, those with the means to do so might be tempted to use it to colonize the past, imposing their own beliefs and values on people who have no way of resisting. This kind of exploitation could have far-reaching consequences for the course of history and the present.

Another ethical consideration is the potential for time travel to create a kind of "temporal inequality." If time travel were only available to a select few, it could create a kind of temporal class system, with those who have access to time travel having a significant advantage over those who do not. This kind of inequality could exacerbate existing social and economic disparities and create new forms of oppression.

Despite these ethical concerns, some argue that the potential benefits of time travel are too significant to ignore. For example, if time travel were possible, it could be used to study historical events in ways that are currently impossible. Historians could observe events as they happened, rather than relying on second-hand accounts and documents. This kind of firsthand knowledge could provide new insights into our past and help us better understand the world we live in today.

Another potential benefit of time travel is the ability to study the future. If time travel were possible, scientists could observe events in the future and use that knowledge to prevent disasters and tragedies before they occur. This kind of foresight could be invaluable in preventing everything from natural disasters to political crises.

In addition to the challenges and risks associated with time travel, there are also practical considerations that must be taken into account. For example, if time travel were possible, how would we control it? Who would be allowed to travel through time, and under what circumstances? How would we prevent abuses of the technology, such as using time travel to rewrite history for personal gain?

Furthermore, even if time travel were possible, it is unclear how we would actually go about doing it. The concept of time travel raises a number of paradoxes and logical contradictions that we currently do not have the tools to resolve. For example, if someone were to travel back in time and kill their own grandfather, what would happen to the person themselves? Would they simply cease to exist? Would they create a parallel universe?

Despite these practical considerations, the possibility of time travel remains an intriguing topic for scientists and science fiction enthusiasts alike. While the challenges and risks associated with time travel are significant, they should not deter us from exploring this exciting area of research.

In conclusion, the prospect of time travel raises significant challenges and risks that must be carefully considered. The potential impact on the natural order of time and space, the ethical implications of altering history, and the psychological effects on the time traveler are all significant concerns that must be addressed. However, the potential benefits of time travel, such as the ability to witness historical events firsthand and prevent disasters before they occur, make it a topic worth exploring. As we continue to advance our understanding of physics and the nature of time, we may one day be able to unlock the secrets of time travel and reshape the course of human history.

In recent years, advancements in quantum computing and wormhole research have sparked renewed interest in the possibility of time travel. Quantum computing, which operates on the principles of quantum mechanics, has the potential to perform calculations that are currently impossible using classical computers. Some scientists believe that this could be used to simulate the behavior of particles in the past or future, allowing us to observe events that have not yet happened.

Wormholes, on the other hand, are hypothetical tunnels through space-time that could potentially allow us to travel to different points in time and space. While the existence of wormholes has not been proven, some scientists believe that they could be created through the manipulation of space-time using exotic matter.

Despite these advancements, the possibility of time travel remains purely theoretical. In order to actually travel through time, we would need to overcome a number of significant challenges, including finding a way to control the technology, resolving the paradoxes and logical contradictions raised by time travel, and developing a safe and reliable method of transportation.

One potential method of time travel that has been proposed is through the use of a "time machine," a device that could manipulate space-time to allow for travel through time. While this idea has been popularized in science fiction, the feasibility of building such a machine remains unclear.

Another potential method of time travel is through the use of "time dilation," a phenomenon predicted by Einstein's theory of relativity. Time dilation occurs when an object moves at a significant fraction of the speed of light, causing time to slow down relative to an observer who is stationary. While time dilation has been observed in experiments involving subatomic particles, it is unclear whether this phenomenon could be scaled up to allow for time travel.

The prospect of time travel remains purely theoretical at this time, the possibilities presented by this idea are too significant to ignore. While the challenges and risks associated with time travel are significant, they should not deter us from exploring this exciting area of research. By continuing to approach the subject with a careful and thoughtful approach, we may one day be able to unlock the secrets of time and reshape the course of human history.

# 11.  Time Travel in Science Fiction Novels

Time travel in science fiction novels has long served as a portal to explore the depths of human imagination and curiosity. From the ancient myths and folklore to modern speculative fiction, the concept of time travel has woven itself into the very fabric of storytelling, offering authors an infinite playground to explore the realms of possibility and impossibility.

What makes time travel such a compelling theme in science fiction is its ability to transcend the constraints of linear time and open up a universe of endless possibilities. Through the manipulation of time, authors can explore alternate histories, parallel universes, and the very fabric of reality itself. Whether it's journeying to the past to witness historical events firsthand or traveling to the future to glimpse humanity's destiny, time travel fiction offers readers a tantalizing glimpse into what could be.

One of the most iconic examples of time travel in literature is H.G. Wells' "The Time Machine." Published in 1895, this groundbreaking novel introduced readers to the concept of a machine capable of traversing the fourth dimension, transporting its inventor to a distant future where humanity has evolved into two distinct species. Wells used time travel as a vehicle to explore social commentary, addressing themes of class struggle, evolutionary theory, and the cyclical nature of history.

Since Wells' pioneering work, time travel has become a staple of science fiction literature, inspiring countless authors to explore the concept in their own unique ways.

From the whimsical adventures of Douglas Adams' "The Hitchhiker's Guide to the Galaxy" to the mind-bending paradoxes of Robert Heinlein's "The Door into Summer," time travel fiction has captivated readers with its imaginative scope and narrative complexity.

But time travel is more than just a narrative device; it's also a philosophical and scientific puzzle that raises profound questions about the nature of time and the human condition. Theoretical physicists have long speculated about the possibility of time travel, exploring concepts such as wormholes, closed timelike curves, and the theory of relativity. While time travel remains firmly in the realm of science fiction for now, it offers fertile ground for philosophical inquiry, prompting us to contemplate the nature of causality, free will, and the very fabric of reality itself.

Ethical dilemmas and moral quandaries are also central to many time travel narratives, as characters grapple with the consequences of their actions and the choices that shape their destiny. Whether it's the temptation to alter the past for personal gain or the responsibility of safeguarding the future, characters must navigate the complexities of temporal manipulation and confront the ethical dimensions of their decisions. From the classic paradoxes of the grandfather paradox and the bootstrap paradox to more nuanced explorations of justice and accountability, time travel fiction forces us to confront the complexities of our own moral compass and the choices that shape our destiny.

Time travel in science fiction novels offers a rich tapestry of exploration and discovery, inviting readers to journey across the vast expanse of time and space in search of answers to the most fundamental questions of existence. From its humble origins in the works of H.G. Wells to its modern manifestations in contemporary literature, time travel continues to captivate our imagination, challenging us to contemplate the mysteries of the universe and our place within it. As we embark on these literary voyages of temporal exploration, we are reminded that while the past may be immutable and the future uncertain, the journey itself is what truly matters, for it is in the act of exploration that we discover the true depths of our own humanity.

Time travel in science fiction novels has a profound impact on both the imagination of readers and the exploration of fundamental concepts that define our understanding of the universe. Beyond its role as a narrative device, time travel serves as a gateway to philosophical inquiry, scientific speculation, and existential reflection. With each turn of the page, readers are invited to embark on a journey through time and space, challenging their perceptions of reality and prompting them to contemplate the mysteries of existence.

One of the most intriguing aspects of time travel fiction is its ability to blur the boundaries between past, present, and future, inviting readers to reconsider the linear progression of time. Through the manipulation of temporal causality, authors explore the notion that every action has far-reaching consequences, rippling across the fabric of time like waves in a cosmic ocean. By presenting alternate timelines and divergent realities, time travel narratives compel readers to confront the fragility of fate and the profound implications of choice.

Time travel fiction serves as a crucible for examining the nature of identity and the essence of what it means to be human. Characters who journey through time often confront versions of themselves at different stages of their lives, prompting existential questions about the continuity of self and the fluidity of consciousness. Through these encounters, readers are challenged to consider the complexities of personal identity and the ways in which our experiences shape who we are.

Time travel narratives provide a fertile ground for exploring ethical dilemmas and moral quandaries, as characters grapple with the consequences of altering the past or shaping the future. Whether it's the temptation to rewrite history for personal gain or the responsibility of preserving the integrity of the timeline, characters must navigate the complexities of temporal manipulation and confront the ethical dimensions of their choices. Through these narratives, readers are invited to reflect on the principles that guide their own actions and the weight of moral responsibility in a world shaped by the currents of time.

Time travel fiction offers readers a window into the wonders of scientific speculation and the mysteries of the cosmos. Authors draw on cutting-edge theories from fields such as quantum physics, cosmology, and philosophy of time to craft narratives that push the boundaries of human understanding. Through thought experiments and speculative scenarios, readers are invited to contemplate the nature of time itself, pondering the possibility of parallel universes, closed timelike curves, and the elusive nature of causality.

Time travel in science fiction novels represents a convergence of storytelling and intellectual exploration, inviting readers on a journey through the vast expanse of time and space. Through its imaginative narratives and philosophical depth, time travel fiction challenges readers to confront the mysteries of existence, grapple with the complexities of identity and morality, and contemplate the infinite possibilities that lie beyond the constraints of linear time. As we embark on these literary voyages of temporal exploration, we are reminded that while the future may be uncertain and the past immutable, the journey itself is what truly matters, guiding us to a deeper understanding of ourselves and the universe we inhabit.

Time travel in science fiction novels has evolved from a simple plot device to a sophisticated exploration of complex themes and ideas that resonate deeply with readers. Authors have used the concept of temporal manipulation to delve into the intricacies of human nature, the nature of reality, and the very fabric of existence itself. With each new story, readers are transported to worlds both familiar and fantastical, where the boundaries of time and space are blurred, and the possibilities are endless.

One of the most compelling aspects of time travel fiction is its ability to challenge our perceptions of cause and effect, offering a unique perspective on the interconnectedness of past, present, and future. Through the lens of temporal manipulation, authors explore the notion that every action has consequences, rippling across the fabric of time in unpredictable ways. Whether it's the butterfly effect in Ray Bradbury's "A Sound of Thunder" or the grandfather paradox in H.G. Wells' "The Time Machine," time travel narratives force readers to confront the implications of their choices and the fragility of fate.

Time travel fiction serves as a vehicle for examining the nature of identity and the passage of time. Characters who journey through time often confront versions of themselves at different stages of their lives, prompting existential questions about the nature of self and the fluidity of consciousness. Through these encounters, readers are invited to contemplate the complexities of personal identity and the ways in which our experiences shape who we are.

Time travel fiction also offers readers a glimpse into the wonders of scientific speculation and the mysteries of the cosmos. Authors draw on cutting-edge theories from fields such as quantum physics, cosmology, and philosophy of time to craft narratives that push the boundaries of human understanding. Through thought-provoking scenarios and speculative adventures, readers are invited to contemplate the nature of time itself, pondering the possibility of parallel universes, closed timelike curves, and the elusive nature of causality.

Time travel in science fiction novels represents a fusion of imagination and intellect, inviting readers on a journey through the depths of time and space. Through its rich narratives and thought-provoking themes, time travel fiction challenges readers to confront the mysteries of existence, grapple with the complexities of identity and morality, and contemplate the infinite possibilities that lie beyond the confines of linear time. As we embark on these literary odysseys of temporal exploration, we are reminded that while the past may be immutable and the future uncertain, the journey itself is what truly matters, guiding us to a deeper understanding of ourselves and the universe we inhabit.

# 12.    Time Travel in Science Fiction Movies and TV Series

Time travel has been a recurring theme in science fiction movies and TV series, captivating audiences with its tantalizing possibilities and mind-bending paradoxes. From iconic classics to modern blockbusters, the concept of temporal manipulation has provided filmmakers with a rich canvas to explore themes of identity, destiny, and the nature of reality itself.

One of the earliest and most influential depictions of time travel in cinema is found in the 1960 film "The Time Machine," based on the novel by H.G. Wells. Directed by George Pal, this adaptation follows the journey of a Victorian inventor who builds a machine capable of traveling through time. As he ventures into the distant future, he encounters a world divided into two distinct species: the gentle Eloi and the savage Morlocks. Through the protagonist's journey, the film explores themes of social commentary, evolution, and the cyclical nature of history, cementing its status as a classic of the genre.

In the realm of television, time travel has been a recurring motif in numerous series, from the whimsical adventures of "Doctor Who" to the gripping drama of "12 Monkeys." "Doctor Who," which first premiered in 1963, follows the adventures of the Doctor, a Time Lord from the planet Gallifrey who travels through time and space in the TARDIS, a time machine disguised as a British police box. Over the course of the series, the Doctor and their companions encounter historical figures, futuristic civilizations, and alien threats, exploring themes of morality, compassion, and the consequences of one's actions.

In more recent years, time travel has become a popular trope in mainstream cinema, with films such as "Back to the Future," "The Terminator," and "Looper" captivating audiences with their imaginative storytelling and dazzling special effects. "Back to the Future," directed by Robert Zemeckis, follows the adventures of Marty McFly, a teenager who accidentally travels back in time to the 1950s and must ensure that his parents fall in love to preserve his own existence. The film's blend of humor, heart, and thrilling action made it an instant classic, spawning two sequels and inspiring countless imitators.

Similarly, "The Terminator," directed by James Cameron, explores the consequences of time travel through the story of a cyborg assassin sent back in time to kill the mother of the future leader of the human resistance. The film's innovative blend of sci-fi, action, and suspense helped launch the careers of its stars, Arnold Schwarzenegger and Linda Hamilton, and solidified its status as a cultural phenomenon.

In the realm of television, "12 Monkeys," inspired by the 1995 film of the same name, follows the journey of a time traveler from a post-apocalyptic future who is sent back in time to prevent the outbreak of a deadly virus that will decimate humanity. As he navigates the complexities of time travel and the machinations of a mysterious organization known as the Army of the 12 Monkeys, he grapples with questions of fate, free will, and the nature of reality itself. The series received critical acclaim for its complex storytelling, compelling characters, and thought-provoking themes, cementing its status as one of the most ambitious time travel narratives in recent memory.

Time travel in science fiction movies and TV series offers a rich tapestry of exploration and discovery, inviting audiences to journey across the vast expanse of time and space in search of answers to the most fundamental questions of existence. From the classic adventures of "The Time Machine" to the modern thrills of "Doctor Who" and "12 Monkeys," time travel continues to captivate our imagination, challenging us to contemplate the mysteries of the universe and our place within it. As we embark on these cinematic journeys of temporal exploration, we are reminded that while the past may be immutable and the future uncertain, the journey itself is what truly matters, for it is in the act of exploration that we discover the true depths of our own humanity.

Time travel has become a staple of science fiction storytelling in both movies and television series, captivating audiences with its ability to explore the complexities of time, space, and human existence. From mind-bending plot twists to thought-provoking philosophical dilemmas, time travel narratives offer a rich tapestry of exploration and discovery that continues to fascinate viewers of all ages.

One of the most enduring and beloved time travel franchises in cinema history is "Back to the Future." Directed by Robert Zemeckis and released in 1985, the film follows the adventures of Marty McFly, a high school student who accidentally travels back in time to the 1950s in a DeLorean time machine created by his eccentric friend, Dr. Emmett Brown. As Marty navigates the challenges of the past and tries to ensure his own existence by engineering his parents' romance, he learns valuable lessons about courage, determination, and the importance of family. "Back to the Future" struck a chord with audiences worldwide, spawning two sequels and earning a permanent place in pop culture history.

Another iconic time travel film is "The Terminator," directed by James Cameron and released in 1984. In this dystopian sci-fi thriller, a cyborg assassin, played by Arnold Schwarzenegger, is sent back in time from a post-apocalyptic future to kill Sarah Connor, the mother of the future leader of the human resistance. The film's innovative blend of action, suspense, and cutting-edge special effects helped establish Schwarzenegger as a Hollywood superstar and solidified Cameron's reputation as a visionary filmmaker. "The Terminator" spawned multiple sequels and spin-offs, cementing its status as one of the most influential sci-fi franchises of all time.

On the small screen, time travel has been a recurring theme in numerous television series, from the whimsical adventures of "Doctor Who" to the complex narratives of "Lost" and "Dark." "Doctor Who," which first premiered on British television in 1963, follows the adventures of the Doctor, a Time Lord from the planet Gallifrey who travels through time and space in the TARDIS, a time machine disguised as a British police box. Over the decades, the series has tackled a wide range of social, political, and ethical issues, while also entertaining audiences with its imaginative storytelling and colorful characters.

In more recent years, time travel has been explored in serialized dramas such as "12 Monkeys" and "Dark." "12 Monkeys," inspired by the 1995 film of the same name, follows a time traveler from a post-apocalyptic future who is sent back in time to prevent a deadly virus from wiping out humanity. As he navigates the complexities of time travel and battles against a shadowy organization known as the

Army of the 12 Monkeys, he discovers shocking truths about his own past and the fate of the world. "Dark," a German-language series created by Baran bo Odar and Jantje Friese, explores the interconnected lives of four families in the small town of Winden as they grapple with the consequences of time travel and the dark secrets buried beneath the surface of their seemingly idyllic community. With its intricate plot twists, complex characters, and atmospheric setting, "Dark" has earned critical acclaim and a devoted fan base around the world.

Time travel continues to be a powerful and enduring trope in science fiction storytelling, captivating audiences with its imaginative possibilities and thought-provoking themes. Whether it's the high-octane action of "Back to the Future" or the mind-bending mysteries of "Dark," time travel narratives offer a thrilling journey through the twists and turns of time itself, inviting viewers to ponder the mysteries of existence and the choices that shape our destiny. As we embark on these cinematic and televised adventures of temporal exploration, we are reminded that while the past may be immutable and the future uncertain, the journey itself is what truly matters, for it is in the act of exploration that we discover the true depths of our own humanity.

As the realm of time travel in science fiction expands, filmmakers and television creators have continued to push the boundaries of storytelling, introducing new twists, ethical dilemmas, and narrative complexities. The ever-evolving landscape of time travel narratives not only reflects our fascination with the unknown but also serves as a mirror to explore profound questions about human nature, the consequences of our actions, and the very fabric of reality.

One notable example of a recent time travel phenomenon is the Netflix series "Stranger Things." While primarily known for its supernatural and horror elements, the show incorporates time travel into its intricate plotline. Without delving into spoilers, the series weaves a tale of parallel dimensions, temporal displacement, and the interconnectedness of characters across different timelines. "Stranger Things" demonstrates the versatility of time travel as a narrative device, seamlessly blending it with other genre elements to create a unique and engaging storyline.

The Marvel Cinematic Universe (MCU) has also embraced time travel in its storytelling, notably in the film "Avengers: Endgame." In this blockbuster, the Avengers embark on a time-traveling mission to undo the catastrophic events of the past. The film explores the consequences of altering timelines, presenting characters with moral choices and dilemmas that resonate throughout the broader Marvel universe. The incorporation of time travel in a superhero context adds a layer of complexity to the narrative, challenging characters and audiences alike to grapple with the ramifications of manipulating time.

In the realm of animated storytelling, the popular series "Rick and Morty" takes a humorous yet thought-provoking approach to time travel. Created by Justin Roiland and Dan Harmon, the show follows the interdimensional adventures of an eccentric scientist, Rick, and his grandson, Morty. The series delves into the absurdities and paradoxes of time travel, often subverting traditional tropes and embracing the chaotic nature of temporal manipulation. "Rick and Morty" exemplifies how time travel can be used not only for narrative exploration but also as a tool for satire and comedic commentary.

The concept of time loops, where characters find themselves repeating the same events over and over, has also become a prominent theme in both movies and TV series. "Groundhog Day," a classic film starring Bill Murray, popularized the idea of a character reliving the same day repeatedly. More recently, the film "Palm Springs" and the TV series "Russian Doll" have reimagined the time loop trope with a fresh perspective, exploring existential questions, personal growth, and the search for meaning within the confines of a repeating temporal cycle.

While time travel often serves as a backdrop for thrilling adventures and mind-bending narratives, it also provides a platform for exploring profound philosophical questions. The nature of causality, free will, and the concept of destiny are intricately woven into the fabric of time travel stories. Authors and creators leverage these narratives to invite audiences to ponder the intricacies of human agency, the impact of individual choices, and the inherent unpredictability of the future.

As technology and storytelling techniques advance, the portrayal of time travel in movies and TV series continues to evolve. Virtual reality experiences, interactive storytelling, and immersive narratives offer new avenues for audiences to engage with temporal exploration. These innovations not only enhance the viewing experience but also challenge storytellers to push the boundaries of creativity and narrative complexity.

Time travel remains a captivating and versatile theme in science fiction movies and TV series. From classic films like "The Time Machine" to contemporary series like "Stranger Things" and "Rick and Morty," the concept of temporal manipulation continues to inspire creators to explore the mysteries of time and the human experience. As audiences embark on these temporal journeys, they are invited not only to witness thrilling adventures but also to contemplate the profound questions that arise when traversing the boundless expanse of time itself.

In recent years, time travel narratives have also embraced diverse perspectives and cultural influences, reflecting a growing awareness of the interconnectedness of global storytelling. Projects like "About Time," a South Korean television series, and "Mirage," a Spanish film, showcase how different cultures interpret and explore the concept of temporal manipulation. These international productions offer fresh insights into the universal themes of love, loss, and redemption, while also highlighting the unique cultural contexts in which these stories unfold.

Furthermore, advancements in storytelling technology have allowed for increasingly immersive and interactive experiences that blur the lines between fiction and reality. Virtual reality (VR) platforms offer users the opportunity to step into the shoes of time travelers, experiencing firsthand the thrill of exploring distant worlds and altering the course of history. Interactive storytelling apps and augmented reality (AR) experiences provide audiences with new ways to engage with time travel narratives, allowing them to shape the outcome of the story through their choices and actions.

In addition to traditional narrative formats, time travel has also permeated other forms of media, including video games and graphic novels. Games like "Life is Strange" and "Chrono Trigger" offer players the chance to manipulate time within interactive virtual worlds, exploring branching narratives and multiple timelines. Graphic novels such as "Watchmen" and "The Infinity Gauntlet" use the visual medium to depict the complexities of time travel in stunning detail, combining intricate artwork with thought-provoking storytelling to create immersive reading experiences.

Beyond entertainment, time travel narratives have also inspired scientific inquiry and philosophical discourse. Theoretical physicists continue to explore the feasibility of time travel through thought experiments and mathematical models, grappling with questions of causality, paradoxes, and the nature of spacetime. Philosophers engage with time travel narratives to ponder fundamental questions about the nature of reality, consciousness, and the human experience, drawing on insights from literature, psychology, and metaphysics to deepen our understanding of the temporal dimension.

Ultimately, time travel in movies, TV series, and other forms of media serves as a reflection of our collective fascination with the unknown and the timeless quest for meaning and understanding. Whether exploring the mysteries of the past, navigating the uncertainties of the future, or contemplating the enigma of existence itself, time travel narratives continue to captivate audiences around the world, inviting us to embark on thrilling adventures and philosophical journeys through the boundless expanse of time. As we immerse ourselves in these temporal odysseys, we are reminded of the enduring power of storytelling to illuminate the mysteries of the universe and awaken our sense of wonder and curiosity about the world around us.

Time travel has transcended its status as a mere narrative device; it has become a cultural phenomenon, influencing not just entertainment but also shaping our collective imagination and understanding of the world. From the exploration of time loops in "Groundhog Day" to the mind-bending complexities of alternate timelines in "The Matrix" franchise, time travel has become a pervasive theme that resonates across genres and mediums.

In literature, authors continue to push the boundaries of time travel storytelling, experimenting with narrative structures, character development, and thematic exploration. Novels like "The Time Traveler's Wife" by Audrey Niffenegger and "11/22/63" by Stephen King offer deeply personal and emotionally resonant portrayals of time travelers grappling with love, loss, and the consequences of their actions. These stories remind us that while time travel may be a fantastical concept, its impact on the human experience is profoundly real.

In the realm of visual storytelling, filmmakers and television creators are constantly innovating to bring time travel narratives to life in new and exciting ways. Whether it's the high-stakes action of "Avengers: Endgame" or the intimate character drama of "About Time," filmmakers use a variety of cinematic techniques, including special effects, cinematography, and sound design, to immerse audiences in the temporal adventures of their characters. These visual spectacles not only entertain but also challenge viewers to question their assumptions about time, reality, and the nature of existence.

Time travel has also found its way into popular culture through memes, fan theories, and online communities dedicated to dissecting and discussing the intricacies of time travel narratives. From heated debates over the mechanics of time loops to elaborate fan fiction exploring alternate timelines, the internet has become a vibrant hub for time travel enthusiasts to share their passion and speculation about their favorite stories.

Moreover, time travel has become a potent metaphor for the human condition, serving as a lens through which we can explore timeless themes of regret, redemption, and the search for meaning in a chaotic world. Characters who embark on temporal journeys often undergo profound transformations, confronting their past traumas, overcoming their present challenges, and embracing their future selves with newfound wisdom and insight.

In essence, time travel in movies, TV series, literature, and popular culture at large represents more than just a storytelling trope; it's a reflection of our collective fascination with the mysteries of time and the human experience. Whether we're voyaging to the past, the future, or alternate dimensions, time travel narratives invite us to explore the depths of our imagination, confront the complexities of our existence, and ponder the eternal question: What if? As long as we continue to dream and wonder about the possibilities of time travel, its influence on our culture and our lives will remain timeless.

Time travel in science fiction movies and TV series has evolved into a multifaceted storytelling device that transcends mere entertainment, delving deep into philosophical, ethical, and existential questions that resonate with audiences on a profound level. This genre has continually reinvented itself, offering fresh perspectives and innovative approaches to the concept of temporal manipulation.

One notable aspect of time travel narratives is their ability to challenge our perceptions of reality and the nature of existence. By exploring the possibility of altering the past or glimpsing into the future, these stories invite viewers to contemplate the fluidity of time and the potential consequences of our choices. Films like "Interstellar" and "Arrival" use time travel as a means to explore complex scientific concepts such as relativity and the nature of time itself, prompting audiences to reconsider their understanding of the universe and their place within it.

Time travel stories also provide a rich tapestry for exploring the human condition, examining themes such as love, loss, and the passage of time. In movies like "Eternal Sunshine of the Spotless Mind" and "The Butterfly Effect," characters grapple with the consequences of their actions and the impact of their relationships across different points in time. These narratives remind us that while the concept of time travel may be fantastical, its exploration of human emotions and experiences is deeply relatable and emotionally resonant.

Furthermore, time travel serves as a powerful tool for social commentary, allowing filmmakers and TV creators to explore issues of history, identity, and cultural change. Projects like "Black Mirror: Bandersnatch" and "Watchmen" use time travel as a means to explore the cyclical nature of society and the ways in which past events continue to shape the present. By highlighting the interconnectedness of past, present, and future, these stories challenge viewers to confront uncomfortable truths about the world we live in and the legacies we inherit.

Time travel narratives also provide fertile ground for exploring ethical dilemmas and moral quandaries. Films like "Looper" and "Predestination" grapple with questions of free will, determinism, and the implications of altering the course of history. These stories force audiences to consider the consequences of their actions and the ethical responsibilities that come with the power to manipulate time.

Moreover, time travel has become a vehicle for cultural exploration and representation, with filmmakers and TV creators incorporating diverse perspectives and voices into their storytelling. Projects like "See You Yesterday" and "Counterpart" feature protagonists from marginalized communities navigating the complexities of time travel, offering fresh insights into the genre and expanding its narrative possibilities.

In conclusion, time travel in science fiction movies and TV series continues to captivate audiences with its imaginative storytelling, thought-provoking themes, and innovative approaches to the concept of temporal manipulation. From philosophical inquiries to emotional journeys and social commentary, these narratives invite viewers to embark on thrilling adventures through the boundless expanse of time, challenging us to confront the mysteries of existence and the complexities of the human experience. As we continue to explore the possibilities of time travel on screen, we are reminded of its enduring power to inspire, provoke, and illuminate our understanding of the world around us.

# References:


**References: Fiction**

"11/22/63" by Stephen King

"A Sound of Thunder and Other Stories" by Ray Bradbury

"All Our Wrong Todays" by Elan Mastai

"Blackout" by Connie Willis

"Do Androids Dream of Electric Sheep?" by Philip K. Dick

"How to Live Safely in a Science Fictional Universe" by Charles Yu

"Kindred" by Octavia E. Butler

"Life After Life" by Kate Atkinson

"Making History" by Stephen Fry

"Millennium" by John Varley

"Outlander" by Diana Gabaldon

"Paradox Bound" by Peter Clines

"Replay" by Ken Grimwood

"Slaughterhouse-Five" by Kurt Vonnegut

"The Anubis Gates" by Tim Powers

"The End of Eternity" by Isaac Asimov

"The Man Who Folded Himself" by David Gerrold

"The Map of Time" by Félix J. Palma

"The Shining Girls" by Lauren Beukes

"The Time Machine" by H.G. Wells

"The Time Traveler's Wife" by Audrey Niffenegger

"The Time Ships" by Stephen Baxter

"Time and Again" by Jack Finney

"Timequake" by Kurt Vonnegut

"Timeline" by Michael Crichton

## References: Nonfiction

"Einstein's Dreams" by Alan Lightman

"From Eternity to Here: The Quest for the Ultimate Theory of Time" by Sean Carroll

"How to Build a Time Machine" by Paul Davies

"Parallel Worlds: A Journey Through Creation, Higher Dimensions, and the Future of the Cosmos" by Michio Kaku

"Physics of the Impossible: A Scientific Exploration into the World of Phasers, Force Fields, Teleportation, and Time Travel" by Michio Kaku

"Temporal Void" by Peter A. Mersky

"The Fabric of the Cosmos: Space, Time, and the Texture of Reality" by Brian Greene

"The Future of the Mind: The Scientific Quest to Understand, Enhance, and Empower the Mind" by Michio Kaku

"The Physics of Time: Dilation, Time Machines, and Teleportation" by Richard A. Muller

"The Philosophy of Time: A Collection of Essays" edited by N. Lawrence and K. M. Ludwig

"The Time Paradox: The New Psychology of Time That Will Change Your Life" by Philip Zimbardo and John Boyd

"The Time Traveler's Guide to Medieval England: A Handbook for Visitors to the Fourteenth Century" by Ian Mortimer

"The Time Traveler's Guide to Elizabethan England" by Ian Mortimer

"The Time Traveler's Guide to Victorian Britain" by Ian Mortimer

"The Time Traveler's Handbook: 18 Experiences from the Eruption of Vesuvius to Woodstock" by Johnny Acton, David Goldblatt, and James Wyllie

"The Time Traveler's Guide to Restoration Britain" by Ian Mortimer

"The Time Traveler's Handbook: 18 Experiences from the Eruption of Vesuvius to Woodstock" by Johnny Acton, David Goldblatt, and James Wyllie

"The Time Traveler's Guide to Medieval England: A Handbook for Visitors to the Fourteenth Century" by Ian Mortimer

"The Time Traveler's Guide to Elizabethan England" by Ian Mortimer

"Time Travel: A History" by James Gleick

"Time Travel and Warp Drives: A Scientific Guide to Shortcuts through Time and Space" by Allen Everett and Thomas Roman

"Time Travel: A Writer's Guide to the Real Science of Plausible Time Travel" by Paul J. Nahin

"Time Warped: Unlocking the Mysteries of Time Perception" by Claudia Hammond

"Time's Arrow and Archimedes' Point: New Directions for the Physics of Time" by Huw Price

"Warp Speed: America in the Age of Mixed Media" by Bill Kovarik

# Index